PARADISE:
Sanctuary

CURTIS GLENN JACOBSON

DEDICATION

To all the dolphins that suffer abuse and exploitation at the hands of their captors. May God set them free.

CONTENTS

ACKNOWLEDGMENTS

My thanks to the staff at the Smithville Public Library, Smithville, Texas for their unwavering support.

1 BEFORE THE EXPLOSION

Steve Bly walked through the hangar and stopped at the open doorway. He put on his sunglasses, and waited for the private jet that taxied his way.

The hanger doors faced north. Steve stood, In his camouflage fatigues, at the edge of the shadow cast by the bright, rising sun. The whine of the jet engines drew closer. He put on his headset. Then the silhouette of the plane came into focus, growing larger as it neared the hangar.

Steve guided the pilot into the hangar, showed him two closed fists, and then two thumbs down. The engines shut down. The pilot opened the door and stepped off the plane. He handed Steve a sealed envelope, and they exchanged salutes.

"Morning, Joe. How are the skies today?" Steve asked.

"Wide and blue." They shook hands, and Joe went to his office.

Joe was followed off the plane by six Navy SEAL squad leaders, all from the same Troop. Each one handed Steve an envelope, saluted and then shook Steve's hand.

After the last man, Steve addressed the group. "Good morning, men. Welcome to Houston. I'm Commander Steve Bly. I've been conducting this training session for the past five years. Chances are that any of your predecessors that you may know or look up to have probably been through it at least once with a one hundred percent success rate. This is the first time for each of you. You've read the itinerary and know the purpose of this two-week training session, but I'll repeat it anyway.

"My objective is to teach you the skills you need to teach your squads the factors and skills they need for boarding sea faring vessels with the intent to conduct a successful mission, whatever that may be.

"We will review past missions of your groups and others. We will explore unexpected potential hazards and situations. We will then practice these skills on a prepared vessel in the Gulf of Mexico. Are we understood?"

"Aye-aye, Sir," the group shouted.

Steve walked over and opened the cargo hold of the plane, saying, "I never like to start anything on an empty stomach. So if you'll stow your gear against that wall, we have breakfast waiting for us. Gentlemen!"

They got acquainted over breakfast.

"How did you secure a hangar at Johnson Space Center, and why?" Dave asked.

"I have connections in high places," Steve chuckled. "I live three blocks from here. They just happened to have this empty hangar. The only other active aircraft here are the T-38s for the astronauts. It's close to salt water. Besides, I'm a nice guy and they like having me around."

"Can we meet some astronauts?" Collin asked.

"This isn't going to be all work and no play, guys. This morning, I'll give you some literature, and we'll watch a couple of videos. After lunch, we'll take a ride in that chopper sitting out there. After you get checked into your rooms, I'm gonna take you to my favorite restaurant over in Kemah. I've scheduled a tour of the Center tomorrow morning with one of the beautiful, young guides from the Visitor Center. Just to be clear, guys, you'll be on duty every day accept Sunday. On duty, you will be in uniform. Off duty, you will be in civies."

ɞ•ɞ

After a couple of days, they all got to know each other as a group, and Steve began to focus on the task at hand—teaching the young men the tricks of the trade that he had acquired throughout his career. The remainder of the week consisted of class work, lectures and training videos.

The second week mainly took place at the training vessel at the Coast Guard Station at the Port of Houston. By the middle of the week, Steve put the training into motion by deploying the training vessel into the Gulf of Mexico, boarding it from the chopper, and achieving the objective of each mission.

Friday evening, the class was dismissed from its final training session and the trainees went to the hotel. Joe and Steve sat in his office with the customary bottle of Champagne and a cigar.

"I think this is the sharpest group of guys we've had over the years," Steve said.

"No doubt. Their work ethic and discipline is amazing. It seems like the men just keep getting bigger, stronger, and smarter."

"What impresses me is how fearless and cautiously aggressive they are. It seems like each man can see around the corner before actually looking. You know that's a trait that's bestowed, not learned."

"You've always had that, Steve. Few men do."

"You and me both, partner. That's why we're still here."

Joe raised his glass to Steve. "Here's to fighting the good fight." The glasses clinked and they took a drink.

"I don't know about you, but I'll sleep well, tonight."

"Yeah."

"Is the plane ready to go to California tomorrow?"

"Yeah."

They finished the bottle and left the base.

๛•๛

Steve woke to the sound of his phone. "Hello."

"Steve, this is Commander Davidson. We have a serious situation unfolding in your territory."

"How can I help, Sir?"

"You have six of my best squad leaders that you've just trained for such a situation. There are two unidentified freighters approaching the Texas coast—one nearing the Houston Ship Channel, the other headed toward the Aransas Pass Ship Channel. Intelligence tells me that each vessel is malicious in nature."

"Yes, Sir. Go ahead."

"The one at Houston has already entered the danger zone. The Coast Guard has advanced and is preparing to intercept. We have a squad on location. That situation will soon be under our control. The second one, however, is still outside our coastal waters. I'd like for you to take my men over there, to deal with that situation. We have orders from the Pentagon. There's no time for plans, Steve. It's come from the top down to you. You know what to do. You have about an hour to figure it out. I trust and support whatever you come up with. Good luck, Steve."

"Yes, Sir, of course. Thank you, Sir."

He immediately called Squad Leader number one, Collin Moore, at the hotel. Collin was the oldest, longest standing SEAL of Steve's current group. "Collin, Steve. This is no drill. We have orders. You are now the Squad Leader of this mission. Have your men at my hangar, dressed and ready for action, in twenty minutes."

"Yes, Sir!"

Then he called Joe, and they all met at the hangar at the same time. Joe opened the hangar and began to prepare the chopper for flight. Steve addressed the Squad. "Men, take three minutes to stow your gear in the chopper, get some fruit, juice, and meet me in the briefing room. Go!"

As he addressed the Squad in the briefing room, he pulled down a map of the Texas coast and pointed. "We are going to chopper down to Galveston Coast Guard Station, switch over to one of their choppers, and head down to Port Aransas. As it stands right now, we will intercept and board an unidentified freighter in the gulf headed toward the Aransas Pass Ship Channel. That ship must not enter that channel."

The whine of the chopper's jet engine grew louder as it warmed up.

"It will take us ten minutes to Galveston, two minutes to switch over, and forty to forty-five minutes to Port Aransas. We can talk during that last leg. Any questions?"

There were no questions.

"Let's go!"

Just minutes after the chopper left Johnson Space Center, the Houston Ship Channel came into their view. Steve explained to the Squad that a similar situation was taking place there at that moment.

After they switched over to the Coast Guard chopper and took flight, Steve asked the pilot for an outside line. He called Chelsea and Jacob to tell them to get out of town.

Feeling uneasy about the operation, he called Chelsea once

more as the chopper hovered over the stern of the freighter. "Chelsea, I love you," Steve said. "We have fired on the vessel, and there has been no response since then. It is still moving toward the jetties. We have to stop it. I'm with a SEAL team about to board it. I just want to tell . . ." His phone went dead.

2 AFTERMATH

For their own protection, the small coastal town of Port Aransas was closed to outside traffic. The townspeople celebrated the fact that evil was thwarted at their doorstep. They knew they could survive the temporary closure of their town because support and encouragement flooded in from around the country.

Townspeople were happy to still have a town because of the diligence of the Intelligence Agencies, the U.S. Coast Guard, and a few heroic Navy SEALs. While they mourned the loss of a few of their heroes, they were hopeful for a return to normalcy in the near future.

৩•৫

"I've never lived under a curfew," Jacob said. "I hope I never have to again."

"That was a strenuous week," Michelle said. "I don't like being cooped-up for that long. We need to go check on Chelsea, and go the grocery store."

"Yeah, I can't wait to get out of here either. Anthony said the campus is open to faculty. I need to go by there and see if my office survived. Engineers are going through the buildings to make sure they are structurally sound. So far, he thinks the only damage was some blown out windows."

"Okay. I'm taking binoculars, spotting scope, and camera. I'm sure we can see the wreckage from there. Maybe we can go on the roof."

"We'll see."

"Paradise, do you want to go with us?"

"Yeah, I need to see what happened."

Greg and Sheena had returned to Austin to prepare to move to Port Aransas. There were no dolphins in the pen. So the Andersons loaded up in the SUV to leave the house for the first time in a week. The first stop was at Chelsea's apartment.

"Thanks for stopping by, y'all. I've missed you so much. Excuse the mess. I've had other things to think about," she said, and broke down in tears.

Michelle grabbed her and held her tight. "I know, honey. I know. We're gonna make it through this together. Have you heard anything?"

"No. I've been talking to my parents and sister. They're all worried sick for me. Now that all the travel restrictions have been lifted, they want to come see me."

"That's good. We're going to the campus to see what's going on there. Do you want to go? We can probably see the wreckage from there."

"Oh . . ." She started to cry again. "I don't know. Do you think that's a good thing?"

"I know it will be painful, but it may help you through it all to see it for yourself. We'll all see it together. That's the best way."

"Well, let me change clothes."

ৎ৵•৶

When they stepped out onto the roof, they couldn't believe what they saw.

"My God!" Jacob said.

The others kind of gasped and sighed at the same time. The wreckage of the freighter was a quarter of a mile away.

"Oh man!" Michelle said. "It looks like someone picked it up, broke it in half, and dropped the two pieces."

"I wonder were he was?" Chelsea said.

Paradise silently gazed as a tear rolled down her cheek.

"That's a massive operation," Michelle said. "How in the world are they going to get that mess out of there?"

"I'm sure they have a marine salvage company working on it. They know how to deal with that kind of crap. It may take six months or a year, but they'll get rid of it," Jacob said.

"So, Port Corpus Christi is just gonna have to wait, huh?"

"Yeah. There's no other access for commercial traffic. The International Ship Channel isn't dredged deep enough. And on top of that, the Causeway Bridge might not be tall enough on the south side, and they'd have to go through the Aransas National Wildlife Refuge to the north. That ain't gonna happen."

"This is going to hurt Jonathan and the rest of the fishing industry around here. They're going to have to go thirty miles north or south for access to the gulf."

"Yeah. Besides that, our gas prices, all prices, are gonna skyrocket for the foreseeable future."

"At least the ferries are running again."

The three girls stood arm in arm silently gazing at the wreckage. Jacob slowly shook his head and sighed, turning three hundred and sixty degrees to look over the entire area.

☙•❧

They went down into the building to see if his office was affected by the blast, and found Anthony in the hallway.

"You can't go in there just yet, Jacob. It's a mess. Crews are cleaning up all the broken glass and debris. There's no point in even looking in there right now. Give us a couple of days. I'll call ya."

Jacob called Jonathan. "What are y'all up to this morning?"

"We're just going over the books."

"Chelsea is with us. We came to my office to see what was going on, but I can't even get in there yet. Y'all want to meet us for lunch?"

"That sounds like a good idea, about eleven thirty?"

"Yeah."

So, the Andersons took a ride through town before going to the restaurant. As they drove through a nearby residential area, they noticed a small group of people standing in a front yard talking. Out of curiosity, the Andersons stopped to talk with them.

The man that lived there was telling his story of that tragic morning. "I didn't even know anything was going on. I didn't have the TV on. I was just having a cup of coffee at the table with my newspaper, and wham! The ground and the house shook like crazy for a few seconds. It blew my front door open, and all of the front glass into the house. It knocked me right out of my chair." He showed everyone his cuts and bruises. "It even blew those windows out," he said, pointing at his car.

"No cops drove through here warning you people?" Jacob asked.

"Not a word," the man replied.

So they drove on. Most of the small specialty shops had their closed signs on the front door. Some had larger signs that read "Temporarily Closed." A few stores had more elaborate signs, such as "We'll see you after the chaos." The most activity they saw was glass and window replacements. The local grocery store was over crowded. They went to the restaurant.

"I took these pictures from the roof of the institute," Michelle said. "The view from there is awesome."

Jonathan and Mary were shocked at the wreckage. "It's even worse than I imagined," Jonathan said.

"So what's this gonna do to your shrimping business?" Jacob

asked.

"In that respect, it's actually a blessing in disguise."

"How can that be with all the extra fuel it takes just to get out to the gulf?"

"Think about it; shrimpers have been leaving out through this channel since before we were born, and constantly harvesting the same beds year after year. This will give the area an opportunity to replenish itself."

"That makes sense."

"In the meantime, my crews are actually coming in earlier than they used to because even though they have to go further they catch their limits quicker, and the shrimp are larger. So for my business it's a win-win situation."

"That makes total sense. I didn't think about that. Good deal."

"Finally, a silver lining to a dark cloud," Michelle said, reaching over to grab Chelsea's hand.

"Did y'all see the crowd at the grocery store this morning?" Mary asked.

"Yeah! We're going over to H E B when we leave here."

❧ • ❧

The next few days began to look a little brighter for the Andersons and Chelsea. Somehow, seeing the site where they last heard from Steve made it easier to accept the facts, knowing that his heroic acts were not in vain. At least they had a picture in their minds of what caused his absence in their lives, and they began to come to terms with that.

3 THE ROAD TO RECOVERY

In an effort to regain some normalcy in their lives, the Andersons and Chelsea immersed themselves in the DolphinWorks mission. Their lives may have been interrupted by disaster, but their tasks endured. They still had an important job to do.

Greg moved from Austin to a duplex in Port Aransas, and took a position as Chelsea's assistant. They sat on the deck discussing the future.

"So from now on we'd like for the two of you to escort the whales from all the Ocean Masters facilities to Maine and Washington," Jacob said. "Michelle and I will stay here and deal with all the dolphin issues. We'll run the operation from here, and continue to release the San Antonio dolphins."

"Greg, you don't have to worry about Sheena. She can stay with us when you're gone. She's a little sweetheart, and we love having her around. How's that sound to y'all," Michelle said.

Chelsea and Greg looked at each other and agreed.

"I don't know about Greg, but I think the traveling will be good for me."

"I like the idea too. That sounds good to me."

"Chelsea, do you remember that question I asked you a while back?" Jacob said.

"Yeah. I think you can count on Amber when I'm away."

"Good choice. She has already picked up some of the slack around here while we've all been preoccupied."

While DolphinWorks got back on track, Paradise and Jacob got back to their respective schoolwork. Chelsea and Greg were flying whales around the country. Michelle and Amber were taking care of the Port Aransas dolphins and Paradise Cove.

The town of Port Aransas saw a gradual increase in the number of tourists, and as the autumn season wasn't far away, some of the early-bird winter-Texans began to arrive. Stores and specialty shops reopened, and Port Aransas was on the road to recovery.

It had been a month since the explosion rocked the town. Jacob was in his office catching up on his student's paperwork when someone knocked on his door.

"Come in. It's open."

The door opened, and in walked a handsome, young Marine in his dress-Blues. He had a cluster of decorations pinned over his heart, and his white hat tucked under his left arm.

Jacob stood up, shaking, fighting back the tears.

The Marine approached his desk, and put forth his hand. "Mr. Anderson, my name is Sean Bly, Steve's brother."

Jacob's knees buckled as he bent down with his elbows on his desk, cupping his hands over his face, bawling.

Sean went around the desk, grabbed him, lifted him up, and hugged him. He softly whispered in his ear, "He's alive."

"Oh my God! Thank you, Father!" Overwhelmed with emotion, it took a few minutes for him to regain his composure. "Where is he?"

"He's at the Brooke Army Medical Center at Fort Sam Houston."

"Oh my God! We thought he was dead. Tell me more . . . no wait. Can you go home with me? My wife needs to meet you."

"Yes, sir. I know y'all have a lot of questions. Is Chelsea there?"

"No, but we'll get her there ASAP."

So he called Michelle. "I'm coming home. There's something we need to discuss."

"Okay. I'm in the office."

Jacob walked in the back door. Michelle was in the kitchen getting a cup of coffee. "What's that big grin on your face for?" she asked.

"Honey, I have someone I want you to meet."

Sean stepped in the door. "Hello, Michelle. My name is Sean Bly."

She was befuddled, and her knees buckled. Jacob grabbed her, and held her up. "I'm sorry, honey. I didn't know how else to do this. Steve is alive!"

She started crying and trembling. "Thank you, God, thank you. Is he okay? Where is he?"

"He's in Brooke Medical center in San Antonio. Let's sit down. Oh, I have to call Chelsea, and get them home," Jacob said. So he picked up the phone and dialed. "Chelsea, Something has come up here, and we need for y'all to come home immediately. Don't wait for a commercial flight. Charter a private jet, and come home now, please."

"Goodness, Jacob. What is it?"

"Don't worry, it's not bad, but it's too much to say on the phone. When you land in Corpus, just get a cab to bring ya home, okay? Do it now, Chelsea."

"Okay. We'll get there as quick as we can."

"Call me when you get to Corpus."

"Okay, bye."

Jacob opened a cabinet, and pulled out a bottle of Jack Daniels. "Will you join me, Sean?"

"Yes, sir. On the rocks, please."

"Michelle?"

"Yeah."

He poured the drinks, and sat at the table. "I guess you can imagine what we've been going through around here."

"Yes, sir, after finally talking with Steve, I can. I was in Iraq, and didn't find out for a week after the fact. When I finally got to Steve, he begged me to come to you."

"You know you're gonna have to tell this story again when Chelsea gets here."

"I understand. That's fine. Let me tell you his condition. He looks worse off than he is. He's in traction. Most of his body is covered in bandages or casts. He has a broken leg, broken ribs, a punctured lung, a broken arm, and contusions to his head. He was unconscious for three days, but his spirit is perking up a little each day now."

"Why didn't he just call us?"

"We talked about that, but decided this would be the best way. Look, it comes down to this; he doesn't want y'all to see him like this. He's embarrassed and a little ashamed for letting the situation get out of hand. He wants to keep a lid on the fact that he survived. The press must not find out."

"I know Steve pretty well, and that sounds like he wants to go after them. We didn't know he had any family."

"He realizes that. I'm his only living relative, but his secrecy is a product of his line of duty."

"We don't even know what that is."

"Well, he told me to answer any and all of your questions."

"All I know is that he *was* in the military, but what was he

22

doing with Navy SEALs?"

"Let me give you his military background. He was a Marine Gunnery Sergeant and infantry leader in Operation Desert Storm. Then he became a Lieutenant Commander for the Intelligence Division of the Navy SEALs. Now he is a military contractor specializing in intelligence and strategy for the Navy SEALs, answering only to the Secretary of the Navy, the President of the United States, and the Governor of Texas."

"Ah! That's why the Marine guard at Arlington National Cemetery saluted him when he showed him his opened wallet."

Sean kind of chuckled. "You may not have seen it, but that guard probably started shaking in his boots."

"He did stutter a few times. Man! He's a VIP!"

"Yes, sir. He has contacts in every country of the world. Vice President Quayle awarded him with the Silver Star in 1992 for his action in Kuwait and Iraq during Operation Desert Storm."

"I guess the next obvious question is can we go see him?"

"He asks that you wait a couple of weeks until some of the bandages are removed. Right now they have him on so many drugs he can hardly stay awake. He just needs a little more time."

"That's understandable."

"Now I have a question for you. Is it possible to see the explosion site?"

"That's a great idea. We have the perfect viewpoint. Hey, do you mind if I invite my friend, Jonathan, to join us? He needs to meet you as well."

"Sure. I'm here for all of you on my brother's behalf."

ঙ৽•ন৶

They were standing outside of the vehicle at Jacob's office when Jonathan and Mary arrived. Jonathan got out of his truck with a befuddled look on his face, and didn't say a word.

"Steve is alive!" Jacob said.

Jonathan staggered sideways, and Jacob caught him. "This is his brother, Sean."

They stood on the roof looking at the wreckage when Jacob's phone rang. "That was Chelsea. They're in a cab headed home. Let's go back to the house."

It was hard to dampen the celebration, but they did. Michelle kept watch for the cab coming down the street. "Here they come, y'all, settle down."

Everyone in the house heard the footsteps as Chelsea and Greg came up onto the deck. Greg opened the door. Chelsea entered first. Michelle met her at the door.

Chelsea took a couple of steps into the house, and stopped dead in her tracks. She saw everyone just standing there, looking at her. Then she saw Sean. She started crying, and her knees buckled.

Michelle caught her, and whispered in her ear, "Steve is alive!"

Sean went over, pulled Chelsea out of Michelle's arms, held her tight, and whispered in her ear, "He wanted me to finish his sentence that was interrupted. He was about to say, 'I love you, and everything is going to be okay.'"

Chelsea continued to cry for a few minutes, but her tears were tears of joy.

Just then Paradise walked in the door, and saw a celebration breaking out.

"Paradise!" Michelle said.

Sean went to her. "Are you Paradise?"

"Yes."

"My name is Sean Bly."

She was befuddled and on the verge of tears.

"Steve is alive!"

Her knees buckled. Sean caught her and held her. Then she went to Michelle, crying tears of joy.

While the celebration commenced, Sean slipped out the door. When he returned, he had a magnum of Champaign and a box of cigars, and everyone applauded as he put them on the table. The he pulled a sheet of paper out of his pocket, and said, "Steve gave me this mission, which I am about to complete. I need to check off a list of names then read his statement. Please don't be offended if you are here, but your name is not on the list. Chelsea, Paradise, Jacob, Michelle, and Jonathan."

Everyone stood silent.

"He has this to say to you; 'You know I always enjoy good Champaign and good cigars after a successful mission. I lost a few good men this time, but the bad guys are all dead. Although I am not there, I am with you in spirit.' Michelle?"

"I know what to do," she said, and everyone laughed as she got the glasses and an ashtray.

Sean opened the bottle, filled the glasses, and handed out the cigars. Then he lifted his glass. "To those who fight the good fight of good against evil."

The glasses clinked, and they drank. The party was on!

"Good job, Sean, spoken like the master himself!" Jacob said.

"You are going to stay the night with us, aren't you?"

"He told me you'd say that, so I brought a change of clothes." While he was out at his car, he called the hospital to speak to Steve's nurse. "This is Gunnery Sergeant Sean Bly. Please give my brother, Steve, a message from me. Just tell him, mission accomplished, all is well."

Jonathan fired up the pit with mesquite wood. Jacob brought out his deep fryer, and the celebration kicked into high gear. Everyone was reinvigorated by the news that they hadn't lost their good friend, Steve.

Sean was treated like a celebrity as they all got to know him. Paradise took him out to meet the dolphins.

"This is so cool. I've seen large schools of spinner dolphins in the ocean, but I've never seen this many bottlenose dolphins together, up close."

"We started with one. Come here, Sam." She introduced them.

"Which one is Destiny? Steve told me the story about her."

"Come here, Destiny." Providence followed. "These are our only spotted dolphins. They're probably the only ones in the bay. We'll show you some video on these two later."

"Is she going to start getting her spots soon?"

"Probably not for another year, and then they'll gradually increase as she grows."

"She is so cute! What a little sweetheart."

"Yeah, she's also a ham."

"This is a lot of dolphins; do y'all put them in that tank?"

"No . . . well, we can if we need to protect them for some reason. That's for the dolphins that we get from Ocean Masters to release into the wild."

"Oh, now that's cool. Steve mentioned that before, but I didn't really understand what he was telling me. Is that what DolphinWorks is?"

"Yeah. We have five facilities around the country to release captive dolphins and whales. We hope to expand around the world in the near future. Tell me more about Uncle Steve. I call him that because I love him that way. He gave me this necklace."

"That's pretty. I can tell from the way he talks about you that y'all mean a great deal to him. I think he feels like part of your family too."

"Is he going to be okay?"

"Oh sure! You know he's as tough as a mule. He's been shot before, but I don't think he's ever been hurt this bad. It's going to take a while for him to recover, but he'll be back to normal before you know it. If I knew different, I'd tell you, Paradise. He's going to be okay. You can rest assured." He pulled her to his side, and gave her a one-arm hug.

She smiled as a little tear rolled down her cheek.

"I never felt that way before; thinking he was gone. That was hard to take."

"You've never lost anyone close to you?"

"No."

"It is a hard thing to understand. We lost our parents years ago to natural causes. I've lost close buddies in battle. As you grow older, it just becomes a part of life that you have to learn to deal with. It always happens when you don't expect it, and it's never easier the second or third time. I can tell you that each time it happens, it does make you a little stronger, but it still hurts."

"God helps you through it?"

"He does, if you ask Him. I've learned the hard way that whether it's you and me, or those dolphins and fish in the sea, all life is resilient and fragile at the same time. Even the mightiest oak, or the most delicate flower, can withstand the strongest of assaults then succumb to the slightest adversity. We can't spend our lives worrying about these things. Repent often, and trust in the LORD."

They went back to the house, and joined the celebration.

ა•ა

Sean spent the night, and as his brother had done years ago, he fell in love with the laid-back, easy going lifestyle of the island.

"I guess y'all do this all the time?" Sean asked.

"Pretty much," Jacob said. "I don't have to tell you about the salty air—how it has a way to magically cure what ails ya. Combine that with a strong cup of java and your good to go."

"I like the way your deck is in a shadow, and the morning sun isn't slapping me in the face, but all that morning color bounces back to give you a brilliant picture."

Michelle joined the guys with a tray of breakfast treats. "Here, Sean, this will get your motor running."

He grabbed a sausage-biscuit, and refilled his cup. "Are you guys familiar with the Navy's dolphin program?"

"Probably not as much as we should be," Jacob said. "Why do you ask?"

"Well, after learning what y'all do for dolphins and whales, I figured one of your future targets would be, SPAWAR, that's what they call it."

"Now I have to ask you a question, how much do you know about what we do?"

"All I know is what Paradise told me. That pen," he pointed, "is for dolphins that Ocean Masters releases from captivity. And I've seen the news that it's not just one Ocean Masters, but around the country. I concluded that y'all are adversaries of captivity."

"And that's all she told you?" Jacob and Michelle smiled at each other with raised eyebrows.

"Yeah. Why?"

"There's more to it than that. You don't think Ocean Masters, or any other facility voluntarily gives up their trained dolphins and whales out of the goodness of their hearts, do you?"

"Now that you mention it that way, probably not. So what's the secret?"

"It turns out that our daughter is a dolphin whisperer. She can communicate with Cetaceans, unlike you or I."

"Ah, I see. You have the inside track."

Jacob and Michelle chuckled. "You might say that," she said. "She just figured it out last year, and we put two and two together."

"We've always been against captivity, but until now we didn't have a way to do anything about it, other than write letters and make phone calls like everyone else."

"I kind of understand, but I still don't get the whole picture. How does her communicating with the animals make corporate America give up their most prized possessions?"

Jacob chuckled again. "She tells them to stop performing, and they do. Without a performance there's no show, and without a show there's no income."

Sean laughed, repositioned himself in the chair, and slapped his knee. "The big picture just came into view, but I'm wondering if y'all know everything there is to know about my brother."

Jacob and Michelle looked at each other with their heads askant, befuddled. "Probably not," he said. "Are you going to tell us?"

Sean laughed again. "I guess I am." He repositioned himself in the chair. "How do I do this? For years, Steve has worked with Navy dolphins on SEAL missions in the Middle East. They use them to detect underwater mines as well as opposition divers. He always said that he didn't like that because electronic technology could do the same job without placing the dolphins in harm's way. But the Navy wouldn't listen to him."

"Oh my God!" Michelle said. "We had no idea."

"I'm guessing that's why he got involved when he heard

Bandweeny was smuggling dolphins. Then he met you guys."

Jacob looked at Michelle. "That kind of puts the whole thing in perspective, doesn't it?"

Michelle started to cry, and leaned over to hug Jacob. "He's one of us."

"Now, now, Michelle—don't get all mushy on us. I'm sure Steve isn't one of those wacko activists that shows up to every protest to ban this or that."

"Not at all," Sean said. "My brother has always been a private person, now he has to be. I've never known him to worry about the emotional state of the masses just because they don't like one thing or another. I think that kind of crap annoys him, but when it comes to injustice—that's a different matter, entirely."

"I guess that's why we get along so well. He knows we aren't mainstream activists. I've never been to a public protest in my life, but I will stand up and fight for what's right."

"Before all this happened, I last saw him about four months ago when I was on leave. He told me that's what he likes about y'all, you stand up and fight for dolphins, that you don't just flap your gums like an activist, but you actually get things done. Now I understand.

"That's why I mentioned SPAWAR. I just assumed Steve

would have had you all over that one by now. I wouldn't be surprised if they had at least one team of dolphins over at that wreckage site searching for evidence, even body parts."

They both raised their eyebrows. Then Jacob said, "That's odd, he's never mentioned it."

"I guess he's had his hands full lately."

"Can you tell us how he ended up with that SEAL team right over there," Jacob pointed.

"Sorry, Jacob. I have to let him tell ya that one."

ॐ•ॐ

Day by day, Port Aransas recovered from the explosive attack on its quiet, small town, island shore. It was the nature of the resident population to depend and draw on the help and support of their neighbors.

Jacob and Jonathan had breakfast at the little café on the harbor.

"The government did the right thing hiring local companies to clear the channel," Jonathan said.

"Yeah, who knows these waters better than the people that live and work here?"

"You know what I'm starting tomorrow?"

"What?"

"They've got me, and a couple of other guides, shuttling food and water out to the barges. They gave us a tour of the site yesterday to mark all the underwater hazards, and to tell us the *do's* and the *don'ts* in the restricted area."

"You mean you got up close to it?"

"Yeah. It's a scary thing, Jacob. I don't know how much, or what kind, of explosives were on that ship, but that thing is scattered hundreds of yards in all directions."

"Wow! Can you take pictures?"

"The ship was headed into the channel. The closer we got to it; my skin began to crawl. It was like walking through a haunted house—you don't know what's around the corner, and you're waiting for something to pop out in front of you. That's what it was like moving through the debris field for the first time, up close and personal."

Jonathan's voice began to crack as he continued. "You remember the morning started out foggy with a little nip in the air. Moving around that scrap heap that randomly juts out of the invisible depths was eerie. As we moved around the wreckage toward the stern, something came into view that I will never forget." He hesitated.

"What . . . what was it, Jonathan?"

"Off in the distance, behind the ship's wreckage, there was an American flag flying in the breeze. That by itself brought tears to all of our eyes, but as we got closer, I started to make out what that flag was attached to." He hesitated.

"Come on, Jonathan, what was it? You're killing me here!"

"It looked like a black, steel cross, rising up out of the water. Now, that ship isn't sitting in the middle of the channel. It's more to the north side, by San Jose Island, in about thirty feet of water.

"As we got closer to that flag, our escort could probably tell that we were all a little shaken by the sight, and he stopped the boat. He told us that it was the tail-section of one of the two Navy helicopters attempting to drop SEALS on the stern of the ship when it exploded. The other helicopter was below the one, and the two were mangled together.

"Almost simultaneously, we all reached for our phones to take pictures. That's when he politely stopped us, saying, 'Sorry, gentlemen. All photographs are prohibited.'"

"Oh my God, Jonathan! That's where Steve was when his phone went silent! We thought he was dead, right there at that spot!"

"So no, we can't take pictures. They have strict regulations on us. They're gonna inspect us before we enter and when we leave the restricted area, but guess what?"

"What?"

"They asked us to have two helpers on our boats when we enter the restricted area . . . you want to go?"

"Hell yeah!"

"Okay. We'll go over that later. You can help me with some prep-work on the boat this evening. I'll call ya later, and you can meet me at my boat."

"What do ya got?"

"Just some decals and a flag to mount, and I'll fill ya in on what we have to do and how." He pulled some papers out of his pocket. "Here, you need to fill theses out and sign them. You know how the government is—they're a stickler for paperwork."

"What have they been doing up to now?"

"The only people out there so far have been government people—FBI, CIA, Navy and Coast Guard mine sweepers, and divers mapping and marking the debris field, and recovering any evidence they could find.

"Now they're starting the second phase—removal and salvage."

"How long do you think it'll take?"

"Man! I don't know, Jacob. From what I saw, it may take years."

"Oh, man! You're kidding."

"No, I'm not. Of course, they're gonna start at the perimeter and work toward the hull. They told us that when they get to the hull, it is just far enough out that they plan on shifting the channel enough to reopen it to commercial traffic."

"Oh, I see. That's a good idea."

"Yeah, and I think it just might work."

"Well, winter is coming up soon."

"It's code RED, Jacob—twenty-four-seven."

ဆို•ယ

Winter did have its sights on the Texas coastal bend, but first there was a matter of the upcoming holiday season.

Large numbers of tourist and weekend visitors flocked to the quiet, little town, perhaps curious about what had happened. The number of winter Texans grew proportionally to previous years, and the economy flourished as a result.

4 THE HOLIDAYS ARE HAPPY

Greg moved in to a house on Roberts Street. For all the many years he had gone to Port Aransas that house was in the corner of his eye. When he saw that it was available as a "rent to own," he jumped at the chance.

I'm a lucky man, he thought. *What a blessing, not only to move to Port A, but to this house, and to get to work with dolphins, with an old friend.*

It was the only house on the street that was raised on stilts. The split-level floor plan gave the upper half an ambience of a loft. The bedroom window conveniently invited the sea breeze from the gulf to alter its path.

This must be what Heaven is like—the breeze, the gentle hum of the ferry engines, the fragrance of the salty air, and with Sheena at his feet, he drifted off to sleep.

He dreamed of times when life was once so simple. Like his parents before him, he never had much money at one time, but they all seemed to manage their lot in life, making ends meet.

The youngest of four siblings, Greg had been alone since his parents went to Heaven back in nineteen ninety-three—thirteen days apart. He was years apart from his siblings, and they were all scattered around Central Texas.

He had since lost a number of close friends including three canine companions. Still alone, for the most part, his dreams both haunted and comforted him.

Sheena was a blessing from God, Who sent her to him as a stray so that when Missy died, he still had a friend to love and care for— a friend that loved him back, unconditionally.

Greg continued his writing in Port Aransas. He went to bed with the sun, woke up at three thirty, and sat at his computer by a window overlooking his front porch to the streets of the small, quiet town.

What more could I ask for, he thought?

5 A HAPPY THANKSGIVING

The Andersons didn't celebrate Halloween in the traditional sense of goblins and ghouls. It served as the starting point for the upcoming holiday season. Although Halloween wasn't the official start of autumn it did signal the physical changes that became evident at that time of the year, even in Port Aransas, Texas.

"Ah, finally to be able to walk out here in the morning and not have instant sweat beading on your brow," Michelle said.

"It's that time of year, huh? Too bad palm trees don't change colors," Jacob said, and they both chuckled. "Well, there is that one Red Oak in that yard on the way to town."

"Good morning, dear. You gonna have your breakfast on the deck this morning?"

"Yeah. Wow, that's a north breeze isn't it?" Paradise said.

"It kind of puts a little nip in the air, huh? That'll get your blood flowing, wake you up, and get you ready for that math test this morning."

"Don't remind me, Mom. I had nightmares about it."

"Well, you girls have been studying for it. You shouldn't have any problem," Jacob said.

"Easy for you to say, Doctor Anderson. I'm still just a kid trying to get out of high school."

Jacob reached over and patted her on the shoulder. "I'm sure you'll do just fine. Michelle, David gave me something to think about last night."

"What's that?"

"The last two dolphins, to release from there, is an older male, female pair that are beginning to get a little fragile. He held off releasing them because he just didn't know what to do with them."

"What's their background?"

"They were both captured in the gulf by Tampa. They've been together probably their whole lives, which is rare, and San Antonio is their third captive home. Each one is about thirty-years-old. He'll fax you their files this morning."

"Yeah, well, we haven't dealt with any like that yet. We're

gonna have to think about that."

"Mom! Did you forget about Alley? Why don't you call her? I bet she has the answer."

Michelle perked up and smiled. "I think you're right, darling. I'll do that after Chelsea gets here."

ജ•ര

"Good morning, Chelsea. How ya doing today?" Michelle asked.

"I'm great. I love the morning we're having. It's beautiful, isn't it?"

"It sure is. I got some nice fruit and berries yesterday, and your favorite cereal is up there. Help yourself. What do you have planned for today?"

"Boyce is going to release his whales next week, so I need to talk with him about that and make plans to go up there. And then Conrad is releasing his Belugas the week after, so I need to touch bases with him. Then I just need to touch bases with California and Florida to make sure everything is going well with them."

"You still haven't herd from Steve?"

"No, but knowing he's okay makes it better. He'll call when he's ready."

"I'm sure he will. Well, Greg is coming out to clean and inventory the shed and boathouse, and do some property maintenance. We have a couple of dolphins that I want to get your input on."

"From Ocean Masters? I thought there were three left."

"There was, but apparently one of them died from pneumonia, liver, and kidney disease. It just came on all of a sudden."

"Oh, poor thing. That's so sad."

"Yeah, David said he had been nursing her along for about three weeks, but nothing seemed to help her much. She died yesterday. It's that damn confinement in artificial seawater. He's not convinced that she didn't commit suicide. Anyway, that's why he called Jacob last night to expedite moving the last two."

"Doesn't that make you feel great to know that we've moved all those dolphins out of prison to freedom?"

"Oh, to no end," Michelle said. "So we have a male and female pair, both about thirty-something, named George and Gracie."

"That's cute."

"They were captured together as juveniles off the gulf coast at Tampa. San Antonio is their third prison. They need to stay together, but David is worried about their chances, in the wild, in another new place."

"So what choices do we have, I mean between here, California, or Florida, where they came from?"

"Things have changed since they were there. That might be too rough for them now. They need sanctuary."

"Yeah, but we don't really have a facility like that yet."

"We do. It's been here for a long while, but it's new to us."

"Where is it, and how did you find out about it," Chelsea asked.

"That's the interesting part of it. Paradise's Angel, Lucas, told her about it and gave her this card." She handed it to Chelsea. "I've spoken to her once. She's an amazing lady, one of the first women to become a Navy Aviator. She has a Master's in geography and a Ph.D. in Psychology. Most impressive, though, is that she was the second female to go into space on the shuttle."

"Oh my God! Alley Peabody," Chelsea said. "Where is she?"

"She operates a sanctuary for Cetaceans on the Island of Saint Croix, a hundred miles southeast of Puerto Rico, in the Caribbean."

"Wow, you've got me so excited for *this* early in the morning."

"Well, I'm getting ready to call her up. You want to join me?

I'll put her on the speaker and we can both talk to her if you want?"

"Are you kidding? Let's do it, girl."

"You sit down and have your breakfast. I'll go get the files on the two dolphins and we'll look them over so we'll know what we're talking about."

Michelle returned to the table. Greg arrived and had a cup of coffee with the girls, then went outside. They discussed the dolphins and what they needed to find out from Alley. Then they went into the office to make the phone call.

After the initial greetings and introductions, Michelle got down to the basics. "What brought you to Saint Croix, Alley?"

"Well, as I orbited the planet, I began to notice certain places that had a peculiar glow about them, not just in one area or confined to the coastlines, but on all the continents. I photographed and documented as many as I could. None of the other astronauts had ever noticed them before and we had no idea what they were. When I got home to Houston, being a geographer, I had to investigate. Using some NASA resources, I found out that all those sites were animal sanctuaries of one kind or another. I came to Saint Croix for some first-hand knowledge. I've been here ever since."

"That's fascinating," Chelsea said. "So do you just care for Cetaceans there?"

"Not quite," Alley chuckled. "We have monkeys, gorillas, some other jungle species, and a few rehabilitated humans as well. I am a psychologist."

"Do you mean criminals?"

"No, no, let's just say, social misfits. They make up our volunteer base. Without their help, we couldn't operate."

"So you have a small village?" Michelle asked.

"It seems like it has grown into a small town, but yes. We have vegetable gardens, banana trees, chickens, and fishing boats. We're almost self-sufficient."

"So what do you think about our two dolphins. Could they live out the rest of their lives with you?" Michelle asked.

"I would very much love to have them here, yes."

"We have to figure out how to get them there."

"Not a problem," Alley said. "I've been informed about your situation. You live on the water. You've transported many dolphins from inland to your facility, yes? Well, I just happen to have a seaplane that has been modified to transport dolphins and small whales. And I have a very seasoned pilot that I flew with in the Navy, he's my husband."

The girls laughed with joy. Michelle half-laughed and half-cried. "Alley, can y'all come here to pick up George and Gracie?"

"We can and we will, honey."

"Let me think a minute." Michelle started rattling off ideas from the top of her head. "They're still in San Antonio. We'll get them here in a few days. I want to keep them here for maybe two or three weeks to let them acclimate to being out of prison. What do you think?"

"I think you're working out a plan, sweetie. You keep in touch with me. Call me any time you want either just to talk or to discuss the plans, okay?"

"Thank you, Alley. I have a lot of happy work to do. You've made my day."

"Mine too," Chelsea said.

"Well, we all have a common goal, and that makes me happy. So I'll let you girls go for now. Bye."

"Oh my God," Michelle said. "This is so incredible! I have to call Jacob."

"What's up," He said.

"Honey, you have to come home for lunch. We have some fabulous news to tell you."

❦

DolphinWorks was finally active again after all the tragedy that fell on Port Aransas. Steve was alive and recovering in San Antonio. Little by little the town returned to some sense of normalcy, and the wreckage was being removed from the mouth of the jetties. The reopening of the ship channel was within sight.

The next two days were filled with the familiar plans of moving and releasing the final two dolphins from Ocean Masters in San Antonio to Port Aransas. Everyone was excited to get back into the groove of things. Jacob answered the phone.

"Hey, cowboy. You got a cigar?"

"Steve! I got that, and a bottle, waiting for ya. How are ya?"

"I'm ready to get out of this place—that's how I am. What are you doing?"

"We're all getting ready to go to San Antonio."

"Oh, you coming to rescue me from the clutches of these nurses?"

Jacob laughed. "Do I need to bring reinforcements with me?"

Steve laughed. "No, I'm joking. These people have been treating me like a king, but I'm starting to feel like a pincushion. I probably glow in the dark from all the x-rays and MRIs."

"When are you coming home?"

"We'll talk about that in a minute. Is my favorite girl there?"

"Which one? I've got three of them climbing up my back, fighting for this phone."

"One at a time, cowboy."

He gave the phone to Chelsea. She gave the phone to Michelle. She gave the phone to Paradise.

"Uncle Steve, I've missed you so much. I love ya, Uncle Steve. You're a hero. You saved Port Aransas."

"I love you too, little girl. Now, don't go throwing that 'H' word around too much, okay? I still have to finish the job. How are your dolphins doing?"

"They're all fine. When you gave that warning, I went out and opened the gate in the pen. You should have seen Sam, he rounded them all up and led them away from danger."

"That's good. I'm glad to hear that. You did what I would have done."

"When are you coming home?"

"Soon, little girl, soon. Now, put your Dad back on. I'll talk to you later."

"Hey, so what's the news," Jacob asked.

"You really coming to SA?"

"Yeah, tomorrow. We're picking up the last two dolphins."

"Maybe you can stop by here for a visit. They tell me they're gonna let me go in a couple of weeks."

"Sean told us you were in a body cast."

"Yeah. They've reduced that to some bandages and splints. I'm walking around the building. There's a balcony that I go out on for some sun and fresh air, but I tell ya, buddy, I'm going to need a vacation when I get out of here."

"You certainly deserve it. We'll have to think about that. So listen, we'll have to come by early, maybe eight or so because we have to be at Ocean Masters at ten. How's that sound?"

"That'll be good. I can't wait to see y'all. Uh-oh, here they come again. I better go. See ya in the morning."

The next morning, Paradise, Michelle, Jacob, Chelsea, and Greg loaded up in the SUV and headed to San Antonio.

"Mom, isn't that a military hospital? Are they going to let us in?"

"Sure they will. They may have military rules and restrictions, but it's just a hospital. Honey, you told David what we're doing this morning, I guess."

"Yeah. He'll start loading the dolphins at nine thirty. So we have to be there at ten. Everyone help keep track so we're not late."

"Jacob, has Steve told you anything I should know," Chelsea asked. "I mean about his condition or recovery?"

Jacob chuckled. "No, dear, although he did hint that he needs a good vacation when he gets out."

Michelle and Chelsea looked at each other with raised eyebrows.

"Jacob, are we driving the trucks back today?" Greg asked.

"No. David has all that taken care of. They're just using one truck this time and his usual staff will follow along. We still assume responsibility once we leave their gates. So, we have to make sure everything is right before we leave. The girls can check out the dolphins. You and I need to do our own pre-check on the truck."

The conversation continued and varied until they parked at the hospital.

"I'm nervous," Chelsea said.

"No matter what you see in here, he's still the same old Steve we know and love," Michelle said.

They entered the building, checked in at the reception desk, and made their way up to Steve's room. Jacob held the door. Chelsea entered first, followed by Paradise, Michelle, Greg, and then Jacob. Steve stood from his wheelchair to receive hugs from everyone as they came in.

"You look wonderful," Chelsea said. "I thought you'd be all wrapped up and stretched out on the bed."

"I was until a week ago. I'm getting back to normal. So you met my brother. I know you all have questions, so fire away." He returned to the wheelchair.

"How did you end up with a SEAL team?" Jacob asked.

"I've been training Squad Leaders in special situations for years. This particular group was scheduled to leave Houston that day, when I received a call from their base Commander with orders to take them to Port Aransas. You don't say 'No' to a Navy SEAL Lieutenant Colonel or the Pentagon. Our mission was to prevent that freighter from entering the jetties. I guess we did that. Have you had a chance to see the site?"

"We've all seen it with binoculars and a spotting scope from the roof of my office, but Jonathan got a contract to shuttle supplies out to the recovery crews. Michelle, Greg, and I have all helped him several times. It was very eerie at first. They've made a lot of progress."

"I can imagine, and the town?"

"It's getting back to normal. The ferry and highway 361 were closed for a week. We were under Martial Law. Most of the damage was blown out windows and doors. I don't think any structures were destroyed. What do you remember about it? What happened?"

Steve dropped his head and gently shook it. He took a deep breath and sighed. "I've been replaying it over and over, and every time I get the same results. There were nine men on the chopper—a Coast Guard gunner, six Navy SEALs, a Coast Guard pilot, and I sat as a co-pilot. We fired on the deck and bridge to make anyone on board take cover so we could board her. We had no response, of any kind, from the vessel. We took position over the stern for a fast-rope drop to the deck. That's when I called you." He reached over and grabbed Chelsea's hand.

He continued. "That was against regulation, but I had a gut feeling that it wasn't going to end well. So I did it anyway. At that moment, we had two men on the deck of the freighter, one man dropping to the deck, and another beginning to drop. That's about four seconds. I was just about to tell you that I love you when the ship exploded."

"Your phone went dead," Chelsea said.

"The explosion knocked us out of the air, and into the water. That's when time was altered, it shifted into slow motion, and memories begin to meld." The room fell silent. "They tell me things that happened after that, but it's hard to put it together in my mind."

He continued to stare at the floor, and slowly shook his head again. "It's been a long time since I lost a man in battle." A single tear ran down to the tip of his nose. He wiped it off with the back of his hand. The three girls cried at his anguish. No one made a sound.

"The four men that exited the chopper perished. The gunner is up on the sixth floor, in ICU, in a comma. The pilot is in the next room." He motioned with his head. "The other two SEALs have been released." Another tear rolled down his cheek.

"Steve." Jacob broke the silence. "What's done is done. You can't change that. You played the hand you were dealt. You won. You did the job you were sent to do."

"But, four men died at my command."

"They accepted that consequence when they signed on. Those brave men are in Heaven right now with God. They are better off than any of us are. They fought the good fight. They have their rewards. Their death is not a punishment, and you didn't cause it. The bad guys did. Whoever those guys are that caused all this to happen are in total, constant torment right now because they are separated from God's love forever. That's Hell.

"Your four men are celebrating right now, rejoicing! They beat life. God reached down and grabbed their souls before they even knew what happened. They didn't feel a thing. You know that."

Steve chuckled and wiped his face with the back of his hand. "Yeah."

"You'll be celebrating too, as soon as we get you out of this damn hospital."

"I know that's right."

"Steve," Michelle said. "You saved our lives. You saved Port Aransas or maybe Corpus."

"Okay," Jacob said. "Enough of that, Colonel Bly, or whatever you are. When are you gonna break out of this joint?"

The ambience of the room changed.

"Yeah," Paradise said. "Where are you going when you get out?"

"He's coming home with me," Chelsea said. She leaned over and kissed him.

"Well, I can't argue with that."

Greg got Jacob's attention by tapping on his wristwatch.

"Oh yeah, people, we have two dolphins waiting for us to release them from their prison cell."

"One more thing before we go," Chelsea said. "We discussed it on the way here." She knelt down in front of the wheelchair. "How would you like to spend the holidays on a tropical island?"

"I'm intrigued."

"We'll talk later. Do you mind if I call you here?"

Steve jotted down the numbers on a pad, ripped off the sheet, and handed it to her. She responded with another kiss.

"Okay, y'all," Jacob said. "Dolphins are waiting. We know this man is in good hands, so let us away."

ॐ•ॐ

George and Gracie were safely secured in the holding pen of DolphinWorks. Michelle opened a bottle of wine on the deck.

Everyone started to unwind from the busy day.

"I'm tuckered out," Jacob said.

"I think we all are," Michelle answered. She glanced around the table—Chelsea, Greg, even Paradise were all laid back in their chairs. "I'm sure glad we have Amber to take up the slack."

"After this glass of wine, I'll go get some sleep and come back to relieve her after midnight," Greg said.

"I think George and Gracie are the most gentle and graceful dolphins I've ever seen," Chelsea said. "Did any of you notice that?"

"I did," Paradise answered. "They both know what's happening. They're very grateful."

"I have to say that this whole concept of sanctuary for dolphins is satisfying and comforting to the soul."

Michelle smiled. "It kind of puts the icing on the cake, so to speak, doesn't it?"

ஒ•ஐ

The next morning, Paradise was anxious to spend time with George and Gracie. As twilight of dawn began to break, she pranced down to the dock. "Good morning, Greg."

"Good morning, Paradise."

"Mom and Dad are fixing breakfast. They have coffee, if you want to take a break. I'll sit with our new guests."

"Thank you, sweetheart. That sounds good to me." Greg stood up and stretched. "They've been quiet and peaceful all night. Tell me later what they have to say, okay?"

"Okay."

As Greg shuffled off the dock and up to the house, Paradise took a stretch, facing the house, admiring the early glow of the coming sunrise that now silhouetted the house. It was a crisp, clear morning and a gentle fog descended on the dock. She heard a soft, familiar voice behind her.

"Good morning, Paradise. Come sit with me."

"Jarrell, I'm so happy to see you again. What do you think of our two new guests?"

"We are so very pleased with the progression of events that are about to unfold. These two have Father's favor. He is so glad that you took the advice of Lucas when last you saw him."

"You mean the card and Alley. I'm learning to listen to Father when He speaks to me."

"And you are learning very well. He is pleased."

"Jarrell, these are the last two dolphins. What are we going to do after they leave here?"

"Be patient, little one, enjoy your time. Live life as it comes to you. You may soon be in want of spare time. For your future tasks are many, and your time is planned ahead. Your travels will be near and far. Your acquaintances will be great and small, none with lesser value than the other. Keep your head about you. Talk to your Father. Stay in His word. Enjoy your life and the blessings will flow. Fear not, you are never alone."

She heard another voice and turned to it. "Paradise . . . oh, there you are. I couldn't see you in this fog."

When she turned back, Jarrell was gone. "Thank you, Jarrell," she whispered. "I'm here, Mom."

"I brought you some hot chocolate. It's a little brisk this morning. That sunrise is beautiful."

The fog dissipated.

"Yes it is."

"Was that a normal fog or a strange one?"

"Jarrell came to check on George and Gracie."

"How are they?"

"They are calm, peaceful, and happy."

Dawn's early light grew across the sky. Michelle looked around the dock. "All the kiddies are here. How are y'all doing this fine morning?"

Destiny nodded and splashed water with her jaw.

"She wants to go play with 'em. I think everyone's happy today, Mom."

"I'm gonna call Alley today to see if they have a place for Chelsea and Steve to stay for a while. Maybe they could just fly back there with George and Gracie."

"That's a great Idea. Chelsea would go anyway as our representative, right?"

"Ideally, yes. It just works out so well. They could be there for Thanksgiving. Steve needs the rest."

"I wish we could go, Mom."

"Well, your Dad and I were talking . . . maybe we could go see George and Gracie at Christmas."

"Yeah! Please, Mom, please?" Paradise bounced up and down with excitement.

"Don't get your hopes up just yet. We have to see how things work out."

"It'll work out, Mom. I know it'll work out."

ﻦ • ﻦ

The day finally came for Steve's release from the hospital. Jacob, Michelle, and Chelsea loaded up in the SUV and headed for San Antonio.

Steve was ready to go. He had cabin fever. "Get me out of this place!" He said his good byes to the doctors and nurses, and they headed back to Port Aransas.

"What do you want to do first, Steve?" Jacob asked.

"I want to stop in Corpus for a Whataburger. Then go to your place to see the people and the dolphins. Then I want to go to the site."

"I think we can do all that. Of course, we have the matter of a ceremony to conduct. I have all the ingredients waiting for us. The whole gang will be there."

"Good, good. Oh, what a beautiful day."

After a mouth-watering "double-double" with jalapeños at Whataburger, they arrived at the Anderson's at one o'clock to two dozen people eager to see their friend, Steve.

After all the greeting, Steve said, "I really do want to meet George and Gracie and say hi to all the other dolphins." So Chelsea and Paradise walked down to the water with him.

Jacob took the opportunity to gather the ceremonial ingredients on the deck, while Michelle prepared her part in the kitchen.

People gathered on the deck, in the house, down the stairs, and in the yard, as the core of the group sat around the table. Most of them knew what was about to take place. Others had no clue.

Steve raised his hand and spoke. "People, can I have your attention, please. At the end of every successful mission, I like to share good Champagne and a good cigar with good friends. It usually takes place at the end of the mission or a day or two later, but this time I was detained for a while. I want to thank all of you for coming to welcome me back home. It's good to come home. You've warmed my heart to say the least. So without further delay let's get this party started."

He stood, opened the box of cigars, and looked at Michelle. "Michelle, do you mind?"

"Of course not." She got up, went to the kitchen, and returned with a tray of glasses and an ashtray.

Steve handed the first cigar to Jacob then Jonathan then Greg and to anyone else that wanted one. The he opened a couple of bottles of Champagne and poured. Everyone remained respectfully quiet. He checked all of his pockets and said, "I seem to have lost my lighter."

People laughed. Greg handed him his. He lit the cigars around the table. Then he raised his glass and said, "Let's have a toast."

Everyone joined him.

"To the men and women that fight the good fight of good against evil, and to those that have paid for our freedom with their lives."

The sound of clinking glasses filled the air, they drank, and they drank.

Michelle turned on some music. People began to mingle and mill about. The guys stayed at the table, telling stories, one after another.

Greg knew that Jonathan was the pit master at such occasions. He could also see that he was enjoying the conversation. So he asked, "Jonathan, do you mind if I fire up the pit?"

"No, not at all." And he relinquished the reigns of the pit to Greg.

After a while, Steve said, "I want to see it."

"Do you want to go up on the roof?" Jacob asked.

"No, I need to go there. I want to see *it*!"

"We can take my boat," Jonathan said. So he, Jacob, and Steve took Jonathan's truck to the harbor, loaded up into the boat, and shoved off.

Jonathan stopped at the Coast Guard checkpoint at the end of the jetties.

"You're not scheduled to work today," the guard said.

"Do you know who this is?" Jonathan pointed.

"No."

Jonathan motioned to Steve, who pulled out his wallet to show the guard his credentials.

The guard snapped to salute. "Sir! Yes, Sir."

Steve returned the salute.

The guard picked up the microphone and keyed it. "Attention all personnel. Commander Steve Bly is entering the site on supply boat number one. Show your respect."

All of a sudden, horns started blasting in the distance. Steve dropped his head in humility. Jacob and Jonathan patted him on the back.

"Thank you, Corporal. Thank you."

"Yes, Sir. Proceed at your own will, Sir." Again they saluted one another.

Jonathan idled through the checkpoint. "You wouldn't believe how much mangled steel they've pulled out of this water."

"Man! It looks like God picked up that ship, broke it in half, and stuck each one in the mud," Steve said. He stared at the two obelisk-like structures standing out of the water. The boat slipped silently through the water toward the wreckage.

"The first time I toured the site, I had to have an escort boat. We maneuvered in and around the scattered debris," Jonathan said. "They've been working twenty-four-seven ever since. They started at the outside and worked their way to the two shells left standing."

"Go around behind the stern, Jonathan."

He did, and when he reached an acceptable location he took the engine out of gear and shut it down. They sat there quietly for a few moments. Then Steve bowed his head and said a prayer.

A couple of guard boats approached. When Steve finished his prayer and raised his head, the Guardsmen started clapping and whooping. Steve stood and waved. They exchanged a salute.

"Okay, Jonathan, let's go home."

❧ • ☙

The day arrived for George and Gracie's journey to sanctuary, November seventeenth—Jacob's birthday.

The Peabodys were in flight to Port Aransas. Michelle was preparing a feast. Chelsea and Steve arrived with their suitcases and boxes for an extended stay on the Island of Saint Croix. Paradise spent her last few hours with George and Gracie.

"I wish you guys didn't have to leave, but I know you do," she whispered.

The dolphins nodded.

"I know you're going to be happy there. Alley sounds like a very sweet lady. You'll have a lot of new friends there."

Gracie moved close and put her chin on Paradise's foot.

"Now Gracie, you're gonna make start crying." She laughed, and started crying.

Sam was just outside the gate, chirping and splashing the water with his jaw. The rest of the dolphins followed suit. Two of the dolphins knew George and Gracie from Ocean Masters.

Paradise got on the intercom to the house. "Mom. Mom."

"What is it, honey?"

"I can't stand it."

"What?"

"Keeping these dolphins separated like this. I want to let them get together. Can I, Mom?"

Michelle looked over at Jacob. They both tilted their heads askant. "Hold on, we're all coming down there."

On the dock, Michelle asked Jacob, "Should we let them out or let them in?"

"What do you think, Paradise? Will George and Gracie stay here if we let them out?"

"They'll stay, Dad."

"Well, there you have it. Open the gate."

Sam backed up, and George and Gracie darted out of the gate like they were on their way to a fire. They stopped long enough to mingle with their colleagues then began an aerial display of breaches, flips, and spins.

After thirty minutes, Jacob said, "Okay, Paradise, I think that ought to be enough to let them release some pent-up energy and say their good byes. Call 'em back in."

She did, and George and Gracie calmly obeyed, holding their

heads high out of the water as they entered the gate to the pen. The dolphins were happy. The people were happy.

"Oh, I feel so much better now. Thanks, Mom and Dad."

"I do too. I never thought of that," Michelle said.

The phone rang in the house, and Jacob ran up to answer it.

"Jacob, it's Alley. We're beginning our descent into a circular pattern. We've notified the Coast Guard, and we're waiting for permission to land. You should see us overhead any minute."

"Okay, Alley. You'll see a group of people out on the dock by a boathouse." He ran back outside. "They're coming. They're coming."

Minutes later, they spotted the plane circling high overhead.

"This is exciting, isn't it, Mom? I can't wait to meet Alley."

Chelsea said, "I've got butterflies."

"You say he's a Navy pilot?" Steve asked Michelle.

"Both of them."

He winked at Chelsea. She returned it with a smile.

"Why don't they come on down, Dad?"

"They have to be sure the coast is clear. Gosh, I've always wanted to say that." He chuckled. "Here comes the Pilot boat. He's gonna make sure there are no fishermen or pleasure boats hanging around the shore. You know how people speed around from spot to spot."

The Pilot boat blasted his horn at the Andersons. They waved back. A few seconds later, the plane dropped out of its circular pattern to begin its approach from the south. It gradually descended to just feet above the water. Then it made contact with the water and slowed to taxi speed. As it approached Paradise Cove, the wild dolphins disappeared.

"What's he gonna do, Dad?"

"We have it all figured out. He's gonna nose-into the beach. We have a diurnal Spring Tide today that's low right now. It will be high in about three hours. That'll give us plenty of time to eat, load the dolphins, and I have a fuel tanker coming in a couple of hours. We're all set."

The plane turned toward the beach at a slight angle. At the right moment, the pilot cut the engines and the plane coasted to a gentle stop at the beach.

Greg and Jacob waded out into the water calf-deep as Alley opened the starboard side access door. She hopped out of the plane followed by her husband. "I'm so happy to finally meet you all,

This is my husband, Robert Peabody."

By then, Sam had returned with Providence and Destiny.

Jacob introduced them. "They all disappeared when you came in. I'm sure they'll come back soon, but let's go over there and you can meet George and Gracie."

Jonathan, Mary, Anthony, and Nancy arrived. Caleb came to document the event for the local evening newscast. They all went to the house for lunch.

"Wow, you have a feast here, Michelle," Alley said.

"Well, it's Jacob's birthday. I won't say how young he is." They all laughed and clapped.

"Robert, that's an old Coast Guard plane, isn't it?" Steve asked.

"You're right. That's a Martin P5M-2G Marlin flying boat. There were two hundred and eighty-five built by the Glenn L. Martin Company. That one was built in 1965."

"How much can you carry?"

"We can safely carry twenty-five thousand pounds."

"What's the range on it?"

"It's listed at one thousand, seven hundred and eighty-three miles. So our mid-flight fueling range is Miami."

"Is that an easy stop?"

"Oh sure. We have a regular site that we've used many times."

Caleb asked, "I couldn't help notice the words on the side of your plane. Is that her name?"

"Ah, *DE GEN ACLEEZE*—The Angry Angel. It's an ancient Persian legend." Everyone got quiet. "In B.C. 650, before Cyrus ruled the land, a heathen tribe that paralyzed the population with slavery, idolatry, and infanticide ruled the largest city.

"One day during an uprising by the people, a young man appeared in the street. When the heathens drew their swords against him he waved his arms over his head and they all fell dead. Then he waved his arms again and all the buildings on that side of the street collapsed. Then he turned, pointed at a little boy, and said, 'Come with me, I will give you sanctuary.' The two disappeared.

"The angel took the boy to the north of Greece, where he grew to become the founder of Macedonia. He was the great-great grandfather of Alexander the Great. Alexander returned to conquer Persia in B.C. 330. *DE GEN ACLEEZE*—The Angry Angel— that's what we do, we rescue dolphins and give them sanctuary."

"So you gave it that name?"

"I did. I heard that story when I was overseas in the Navy. It stuck with me. It was only fitting when we realized what we were doing. There is a purpose and place for everything, yes?"

"Yes there is."

"So tell me, Alley, where do your animals come from? Do you seek them out?" Michelle asked.

"Oh no, dear. Did I call you? No, the angels take care of all that. Sometimes, no humans are involved—different species of dolphins or whales show up and stay. They may be dying of old age or have a medical issue."

"You have a vet?"

"We have a whole team. They stay busy. Turtles, dolphins, and whales show up with fish hooks, plastic debris or nets attached to them, and many with propeller injuries."

"What about boundaries and protection?" Jacob asked.

"We have no physical barriers on land or in the water. God does, however, maintain the boundaries. We have watched, from the observation tower, pods of killer whales and shark attacks outside the boundaries, but they never come inside to attack. It seems as though the animals have an intuitive attribute as to where to go or not and how to act. We even have some large resident sharks—they do eat fish, naturally, just like the Odontocetes, but they don't attack other species."

"So you have no fences or containment at all?"

"Yeah, we do on land and in the water, only for animals under medical treatment, but they are released as soon as possible."

"What a wonderful operation," Chelsea said. "I can't wait to see it. How many of these sanctuaries are there?"

"I don't know for sure, but they're all over the planet on every continent—well, I'm not sure about Antarctica."

"What's going on over there at that jetty?" Robert asked.

So they heard the whole story and learned why Chelsea wanted to take Steve away for some rest and recuperation. While that went on, a strong thunderstorm blew in from the north.

"Dear, I think we should just get a room for the night. It's already been a long day. We'll start fresh in the morning."

"Nonsense," Jacob said. "We have a room, and we'd love to have your company. We insist."

The fuel truck arrived. The guys went out to deal with that and secure the plane for the night.

Michelle made reservations at their favorite restaurant on the harbor for that evening. Then she showed Alley their office and their life long work with dolphins.

"It is so proper that we have met," Alley said. "It's like the meeting of two worlds. Y'all are real dolphinologists. Robert and I didn't consider the lives of dolphins until later in life. Both of our careers were so demanding. I guess God put it in my heart while I was orbiting the Earth. Now we are care givers for dolphins and other animals."

"It's funny how things work out. It seems like the older we get the smaller the planet gets."

"After we were married, we lived in Houston while I was in the astronaut corps at JSC. Robert worked there in tactical flight operations. We went to the beach and went fishing in the bays and the gulf. We saw dolphins everywhere, but never gave them much thought."

"Like most people," Michelle said.

"Yeah, and now here we are suddenly intertwined in their most integral aspect of life—the freedom to live life as God intended."

Later in the afternoon, Paradise and Alley spent some time with the dolphins, and discussed their long distance connections and friendship.

The next day started early with coffee and breakfast. It was a bitter, sweet excitement. Paradise went out to relieve Amber, and sit with George and Gracie for the last time.

Shortly after, Alley joined her as twilight made its appearance on the eastern horizon. "My, my. It's lovely this time of morning. I enjoy this crispness in the air, and all of these dolphins lounging around are a sight for sore eyes."

"This is my favorite time of day, when it's calm and quiet. It's very comforting to listen to the rhythm of their breathing."

"You're sad that they're leaving, aren't you?"

"Yeah. All the dolphins that came here from captivity are still here. Some of them go away for a while, but they always come back around. I never had to say goodbye to them."

"I promise you that they will have all the love and companionship they want with us."

"I know."

"Tell you what I'll do—I'll send you pictures and updates now and then so you can see how they are doing. Would you like that?"

"I sure would." Paradise perked up.

"Your Mom and I talked about y'all coming for a visit over Christmas. That will be fun."

"I can't wait for that, as if waiting for Christmas isn't enough."

Dawn broke, and all the helpers started to arrive. The plane was turned parallel to the shore for easy loading. The loading hatch was opened, and the door served as a ramp. All the people's personal effects were loaded first. The dolphins were to be loaded last.

Jacob went to the holding pen. "Well, David, what do you think?"

"They are both healthier than the last time I checked them. I've never seen them this vibrant. They're ready to go."

"Okay everyone," Jacob called for attention. "We've arrived at the final moments. Say your good-byes and get prepared. The last thing we're gonna do is load George and Gracie. We'll let Robert and Alley give that call when they are ready."

"I've called for Coast Guard clearance," Robert said. "The pilot boat should be here in thirty minutes or so. When we see it, we'll start loading the dolphins. After he clears our path, he'll come out here and blast his horn twice. That's our cue."

Everyone milled about, making sure they were ready. Paradise, Michelle, Alley, and Chelsea talked and played with the dolphins. The guys were all gathered in front of the plane, laughing and talking. Caleb had his camera equipment set up to record the event. Although this was nothing new for Alley and Robert Peabody, sending two dolphins and two beloved friends away in a flying boat was history making, in the dolphin release program for the Andersons.

Paradise knew Steve and Chelsea would return, but her spirit was scarred by the feelings of losing Steve in the past, she didn't want to lose him again, and certainly not Chelsea. She clung to Chelsea and Steve as much as she could, holding their hands when she could, and hugging them when she could.

"We're just going on a vacation, Paradise. We'll be back soon," Chelsea said.

"I know, but I miss you already. You have to call or write every day so I know y'all are okay." A single tear trickled down her cheek. "Oh, I almost forgot!" She took off running to the house, returned with a small package, and handed it to Chelsea.

"What's this?"

"Don't open it until you're in the air."

Chelsea nestled the package to her bosom. She leaned over, kissed her on the cheek, and whispered in her ear, "I love you, Paradise." And the two embraced.

There was another conversation going on a few feet away. "Steve, I expect you to forget about work for a while, and spend this time regaining your strength," Jacob said. "There's plenty of time in the future to do what I know you're gonna do. So just take it slow and easy, my friend. Will you do that for me?"

"You don't have to ask me twice. Besides, I don't think that girl will let me get too rambunctious. I'm looking forward to relaxing in the Caribbean. This is a wonderful opportunity to get closer to the girl I love and regain my composure." The two hugged.

"You better take care of that girl or you'll have to deal with me." And the two laughed.

"It's time to get busy," Robert called out as the Coast Guard Pilot boat passed slowly by.

The necessary personnel gathered at the holding pen and waded into the water with the first sling to load Gracie in the plane, then again for George. The process was quick and easy. Anxious anticipation ensued. Another session of final good-byes was accompanied with tears and laughter, broken up by the two blasts from the Coast Guard.

"All aboard," Robert called out. The mooring lines were released and secured. He stepped into the plane followed by Steve, then Chelsea, then Alley. The others backed away onto dry land.

The massive engines of the flying boat fired up, and the backwash of air consumed the spectators. The plane slowly pulled away from the shore and taxied out to position, and with the final wave of the hand, Robert shoved the throttles forward. The plane's speed increased rapidly until it lifted off the surface and rose into the air. Higher and higher it climbed.

The spectators watched as their friends disappeared into the wild blue yonder. Paradise, Michelle, and Jacob stood arm in arm waving as silence fell on the shoreline. They didn't say a word, just shuffled back up to the house.

The plane reached thirty thousand feet over the Gulf of Mexico, headed for Miami. With one hand, Chelsea clutched Steve's hand. With the other hand, she clutched the package that Paradise gave her.

"You okay? You can calm down now." Steve looked down at Chelsea's hand squeezing his.

"Oh, I'm sorry." She smiled and loosed her grip. "I guess I got caught up in the moment." She turned to look at George and Gracie, then realized she still clutched the package to her chest.

"What's that?"

"Paradise gave it to me and told me not to open it until we were in the air."

"Well, we're in the air."

She peeled off the gift wrapping from the box and opened it.

The first thing she saw was a group picture of the gang on the deck, making a toast. She chuckled and handed it to Steve. Then she picked up the letter from Paradise, which she read out loud. "We love you both so much. Take care of yourselves, and don't stay gone too long. Have fun and enjoy yourselves. You're on vacation, remember that! Inside the box of stationary, you'll find two sheets of stamps. So you have no excuse not to write. We want to hear about all your adventures and experiences. Take lots of pictures. Don't worry about DolphinWorks, we'll take care of everything. We'll join you for Christmas. Love ya, Paradise, Michelle, and Jacob."

The home front settled down and returned to business as usual. The holding pen was empty, and all the dolphins had been released from Ocean Masters in San Antonio. Paradise worked to finish her term projects and research papers. Jacob concentrated on his students, while Michelle prepared for Thanksgiving, less than a week away. Greg continued property maintenance around DolphinWorks and Paradise Cove, and writing his novel about Port Aransas.

Michelle went all out that year for Thanksgiving. They had so much to be thankful for—Steve was alive, the town continued to recover from the explosion, and all the dolphins from Ocean Masters San Antonio had been released. There were still other species to release and other facilities were ongoing, but all in all they had proved the effort to be successful.

She was a busy girl. Aside from her own chores and duties, she had to cover Chelsea's duties while she and Steve were away. She was thankful to have so much to do. It made her feel vibrant and useful.

One of the things she enjoyed most was shopping for the holidays—it gave her a much-needed break from the computers and paperwork and still fulfilled the needs of a family function. She loved the ferry ride across the ship channel and the seven-mile causeway into Aransas Pass.

Aransas Pass was three times the size of Port Aransas with many shops and stores. For the first time in years, she bought some new holiday trinkets and decorations. Her last stop was at the H.E.B. where she loaded up with baking goods, vegetables, and the much-anticipated Thanksgiving turkey.

Jacob came home from work. "You went shopping today."

"How could you tell?"

He just chuckled and gave her a hug and a kiss. "Did ya break the bank?"

"I left a few bucks in there." They kissed again. "You want a glass of wine?"

"Yes, ma'am. What's for dinner?"

"I don't know about you, but I had a craving for pizza."

"I think that'll hit the spot. Did ya get me some little fishes?"

"You know I did."

Paradise came in the room. "Did I hear pizza?" She gave her Dad a hug.

"They'll be ready in about twenty minutes," Michelle said from the kitchen.

"I think I have my research paper final draft. Will y'all give it a read?"

"That sounds like something good to do after dinner," Jacob said.

So they all sat together at the table for pizza and the daily conversation. Then Paradise gave them each a hard copy of her paper and disappeared to her room. Mom and dad sat at the table with a glass of wine and read.

"She sure has become a good writer," Michelle said.

"Well, she had a great teacher." He gave her a wink. "I don't see anything wrong with it."

"She got a couple of citations mixed up, but the text is clean."

"That's why I kept you around so long."

"Why?"

"All I have to do is ride around in a boat all day, give you the data, and you write it up to make sense."

"No, that's why I kept you around for so long," she said with a smile.

"Why?"

"Because I don't have to ride around in a boat all day, in the sun, that's how I keep my sensuous complexion." She gave him a wink. "And I get to write about dolphins and whales all day—what else could a girl want?"

ଓ•ର

Robert circled the island of Saint Croix several times for the benefit of Chelsea and Steve before landing in front of the sanctuary compound. Alley motioned to them to put on the headsets so she could give them the layout of the island.

"The island is part of the U.S. Virgin Islands. It's about eighty-two square miles, twenty-two long, and seven wide. That part of the island that juts out, directly below us, is one of the two wildlife preserve areas on the island. That's our compound on the northwestern shore."

"It looks like highways and roads provide good access to the area," Steve said. "It's not as isolated as I pictured in my mind."

"You're right. The public can visit the wildlife refuge and our facility. As we move up the south side, you can see the airport. It's only about eleven miles away from us."

"It's beautiful from up here," Chelsea said.

"This eastern end is flatter and dryer than our side. Now, on this north side we have a beautiful reef if you want to do some diving or snorkeling. And over there is a country club if you want to play some golf—Robert can help you with that, he plays."

"I'd like to play, Robert."

"We'll do that."

Alley continued. "As we round the corner, we'll begin our descending approach. The community down there is Frederiksted. Y'all go ahead and buckle up. We'll be landing in a couple of minutes. How are the dolphins, Chelsea?"

"They look just fine, but I bet they can't wait to get back in the water."

"What's the population of the island?" Steve asked.

"About fifty thousand."

Robert adjusted his heading for the correct approach and descended. The water landing was flawless and he taxied to the pier, where several of the staff waited. He shut down the engines and the staff tied-off the plane. Alley opened the hatch and greeted her friends.

"Chelsea, y'all go on out with Robert. I'll stay with George and Gracie. Don't worry about them. We'll get them out of here right away."

"Okay."

"Just take your personal things with you. I'll have someone bring your bags up after we get the dolphins secured in the holding pens."

Robert led them off the pier to a shaded table on the beach, where a young lady met them with tall fruity drinks with umbrellas.

"I need to go help with the dolphins," Chelsea said anxiously.

"No, dear," Robert replied. "You're off the clock. You are now a guest of the Saint Croix Animal Sanctuary. Please, sit and relax. Alley and her staff are magical with dolphins in this situation, believe me. You can watch everything from here."

She looked at Steve, who smiled, nodded, and patted the seat of the chair—she sat.

"Just like you guys in Port Aransas, she's been doing this for many years, and with the same staff. They know what they're doing. She'll join us in a few minutes, and after a while, when everyone gets settled down, you can go visit with George and Gracie."

She took a drink from the tall glass and leaned back in the chair. The young lady returned with a pair of binoculars.

"There ya go," Robert said. "You can scope out the beach. There's no telling what you might see out in the water. You might see a pilot whale, or an Orca, even a humpback. Welcome to Saint Croix." They raised their glasses and took a drink.

Then a man and a woman arrived at the holding pen in a recreational vehicle.

"That's our vet and his nurse, Earnest and Sophia. The clinic is behind the tree line." He pointed.

"The vegetation is so thick," Chelsea said. "It makes me feel like were alone on a disserted island."

Robert chuckled. "There are people and buildings just a stones throw away, but there's a reason for that."

"Protection," Steve said.

"Protection?"

"Yeah, from weather and people. There are pirates in the Caribbean."

"Pirates?"

Robert chuckled again. "Not like in the movies, Chelsea. They're far more sophisticated these days, but pirates, nonetheless. I've never even seen any, but word gets around. Not to worry, we have an arsenal. More importantly, tropical storms can be pretty strong when they come through here and that vegetation provides a barrier."

Alley joined them at the table. "The dolphins are just fine. They're so calm that George took a nap while Earnest examined Gracie."

"That's funny," Chelsea said.

The girl brought out another round of drinks, and a map of the sanctuary. "Maria, did you meet our guests?"

"Not formally."

"This is Chelsea and Steve. Maria's part of our family, she's been with us forever, it seems. How long to dinner, dear?"

"About forty-five minutes."

"Great. Thank you, Maria."

She disappeared through the vegetation.

"We have a mess hall, if you want to call it that—a dining room if you will," Alley said. She unfolded the small map to show them the layout of the compound. "We have a chef and kitchen staff to provide everyone three squares a day. It's not always fancy, but it sure is good."

Steve began to study the map. "A storm shelter. How many people stay here?" Steve asked.

Alley and Robert looked at each other with heads askant, and said in unison, "twenty-eight."

"A hangar. I wondered about that."

"Have you ever flown a seaplane," Robert asked.

"No I haven't."

"Well, there's no better time than the present. We can just make a quick circle, and you can take her into the hangar. Then it'll be dinnertime. Would you like that?"

Steve perked up. "You bet I would."

The two men scurried across the beach to the plane.

"We'll watch them take off," Alley said. "Then we'll go get you acquainted with your bungalow."

It wasn't long until the plane's engines fired up and it taxied away from the pier.

"Steve looks like he knows what he's doing," Alley said.

"I don't think there's anything he doesn't know how to do."

The engines revved, and the plane accelerated across the water until it gently rose into the air climbing higher and higher.

Alley turned to Chelsea. "You ready to go see your temporary home?" The two girls disappeared into the vegetation.

They walked on the well-traveled path about twenty yards, which opened to a large clearing. Chelsea stopped. "Oh my. I had a picture in my mind, but this is better."

"Let's go this way." Alley motioned. "This is the main compound." As they walked along, she pointed out the various buildings with pertinent information on each one. They came to another short path that opened to a smaller clearing, and they stopped. "Well, what do you think?"

"It's beautiful! Now that's the picture that was in my mind." It was a tropical island bungalow on stilts. Wide steps led up to a full-length deck with a porch swing, coffee table, chairs, and a ceiling fan. The bungalow was constructed with wood and bamboo with a thatch roof. "It's just what the doctor ordered," she said with a large smile.

"Come on."

They went up the steps. Alley unlocked and opened the door, handed Chelsea the key, and they entered. There was a sofa, coffee table, and chairs. Chelsea stood and soaked in the ambiance.

"Do you feel it?"

"I do," Chelsea said. "I feel at home."

Alley started pulling the curtains and opening the windows in the front and back of the room. "The breeze flows right through."

Chelsea walked to her left and opened the refrigerator. There was some bottled water, a carton of milk, some fruit punch, and a bottle of wine.

"I had the girls bring a few things this morning before we got here. There's a coffee maker, and there should be some coffee and sweeteners in the cabinet. You and I can go shopping later, if you want. We weren't sure if you wanted to go all primitive or not, so we left the TV just in case. Here's the bedroom and your bags." She opened the door. "There's a walkie-talkie for each of you on the table. They have a ten mile range. So you never have to feel alone or isolated, unless you want to. Like a cell phone, you just plug them in to charge them overnight."

"This is wonderful, Alley, thank you so much. This is exactly what Steve needs right now."

"I better go to the house and take care of some duties before dinner. You'll hear the dinner bell when it's ready."

"Okay, thanks again."

The next morning, Steve and Chelsea were up before the dawn and walked out on the white sand beach as the sun broke the Caribbean's surface. They made their way down to the dolphin pen to visit George and Gracie. Two overnight watchers sat on the dock.

"Good morning. You must be Chelsea and Steve. Come on out. I'm Angela and this is Rafael."

"It's nice to meet you," Chelsea said. They all shook hands.

"We're just changing shifts. He's been with them since midnight."

"How was their first night in the Caribbean?"

"I think they like it here," Rafael said. He was dark complected, but spoke with a British accent. "Several of the resident dolphins came by to meet them and they vocalized back and forth, but for the most part, they were calm and quiet."

"My God, I can't believe how much clearer the water is than back home," Chelsea said. "I guess y'all know their history."

"Yes. I think it was Michelle that forwarded their records a couple of weeks ago, and gave us updates on their progress in Port Aransas," Rafael said.

"From the short time I spent with them last evening, and again this morning, I think they will have a happy life together here," Angela said.

"Do you know yet if they've eaten any live fish?"

"I heard a few sound-pops," Rafael said, "but I couldn't tell if they actually ate anything."

"We'll know soon enough, I guess." They sat on the dock for a while, enjoying the dolphins and the morning. Then went up to breakfast.

Steve and Chelsea spent that first full day lounging on the beach and watching the dolphins. Alley joined them at the table, in the late afternoon.

"I'm curious," Steve said, "Who is that guy with the dolphins? He's not very talkative."

"Oh, that's Jesse, I don't even know his surname" Alley said.

"Strange story, that one. You're right, he keeps to himself, but he loves dolphins."

"How long has he been here, if I may ask?"

"Well, that's the funny thing about him. All I know about him is how he came to be here."

"Do you mind telling me?"

"About four months ago, we got an anonymous phone call from Nicaragua, telling us that there were a dozen abandoned dolphins in a holding pen that needed to be rescued. The caller said it was critical and urgent."

Steve rolled his eyes at Chelsea. At the same time, his right arm jerked down toward his hip, as though he was reaching for his gun, but it wasn't there.

Not noticing Steve's reaction, Alley continued. "We had to respond. We recruited the services of our local yachting club. It was a huge operation, as you can imagine. Anyway, when we got there, we were met by Jesse and a handful of armed Nicaraguan security agents."

"Wow, it sounds frightening," Chelsea said.

"It was, at first, until we hashed everything out. The agents were there to protect the dolphins and us. It turned out that the dolphins had been smuggled, from God only knows where, by a local crime lord, and were up for sale on the black market. But, the crime lord suddenly closed shop and disappeared."

"And he was in on it?" Steve asked.

"Not on the criminal side of it, but he was paid to take care of the dolphins. He was just a local guy that needed the money. He made the call, and the only way we could take the dolphins was to take him too. So there he is."

"And you don't feel threatened by him?"

"Not any more. Robert has questioned him intensely several times. You will notice that Robert, and a few of our trusted workers, does where his pistol now days."

"Do you mind if I where mine?"

"I think we can trust you, Steve," she said with a wink and a smile.

"Does he speak English?"

"Not fluently. I can see that you're aroused by his story, care to talk about it?"

So, Steve told her about the connection between himself, those twelve dolphins, and the Port Aransas explosion.

As Thanksgiving neared, the chef and his crew prepared an island feast of different ethnic cuisines, centered around the traditional American turkey and dressing.

❧ • ❧

"So, what did she say?" Michelle asked.

"George and Gracie are adapting very well, the Peabodys have an outstanding facility, and Steve is happy and following the doctor's orders," Paradise said.

"I bet it's not forty-two degrees and drizzling down there."

"Nope, seventy-four and not a cloud in the sky, but I like this better, Mom. This is Thanksgiving weather." She gave her mom a kiss on the cheek. "Did you notice this stamp and the postmark?"

"I did. You should start a new folder in the miscellaneous file cabinet to keep all of her letters. Then get back in here, we've got a lot to do before tomorrow. We're gonna have a lot of company. How long did it take the letter to get here?"

"Four days," Paradise said, as she entered the office. "There's a Miami postmark on the back."

"Where's your Dad?"

"He went down to the boathouse to help Greg secure everything."

❧•❧

"They said this cold front is going to be stronger than the one last Thanksgiving," Jacob said.

"I remember, that was a good one," Greg replied. "It hit Austin with a bang. I love it when that happens. It makes for a more traditional Thanksgiving."

"I think we have a consensus on that theme."

"Well, it only stands to reason—after you live through a Texas summer, a strong change of seasons is a welcome sight."

The wind kicked up, and Sam started chirping.

"Ah, right on cue. We came down here just in time. I think we got everything buttoned up, huh?" Jacob said.

"Yeah, that's the cold front, no doubt. It feels great."

"I'm about ready for some eggnog, if you know what I mean."

"Yes, I do."

"Okay, Sam, y'all are on your own. Take care of everyone."

Sam nodded and clapped his jaw.

The guys went up to the house. As he opened the door, Jacob said, "The cold front just hit."

"Right on time," Michelle said.

Paradise opened the door and stepped out on the deck. "It's getting cold out here." She went in and closed the door. "Dad, will you build a fire?"

"I think so, little girl. It's a good thing that we had the chimney cleaned last week." So, he and Greg fetched some firewood and built a fire. Then Jacob made a couple of drinks of eggnog with that special additive, and the two guys sat at the table, while Michelle and Paradise scurried around the kitchen, baking pies and making side dishes for the Thanksgiving feast.

It started drizzling outside, and the windows began to fog. The house quickly filled with the aroma of pumpkin and pecan pies, green bean casserole, potato salad, and dressing, while a large turkey soaked in a brine solution.

The next morning, Thanksgiving, Jacob and Michelle woke at four to prepare for the day ahead. Jacob made coffee, while Michelle made blueberry waffles.

"Brr, it's cold." Jacob turned on the outside light. "Man! It's sleeting. It's thirty-two degrees out there." He built a fire in the fireplace.

Michelle warmed up the oven for the turkey, and they ate breakfast.

"I feel a perfect day coming on." Michelle said.

"It's certainly starting out that way." He leaned over and kissed her cheek. "Have I told you that I love you, lately?"

"You told me last night."

"Well, I'll tell you again, I love you, and our life here."

"We did good, huh?"

"Yeah, we did. We have a lot to be thankful for."

Paradise waddled in, rubbing the sleep out of her eyes, in her pajamas and gown, her long, blonde hair in her face. "Is it Christmas?" She slumped down on her Mom's shoulder and yawned.

"No, Dear, you must still be dreaming," Michelle said.

"It feels like Christmas."

"You want hot chocolate or coffee?"

There was a flash of lightening, and Michelle counted. "Thousand one, thousand two, thousand three . . . ." Boom! "It's almost on top of us."

Paradise stood up, waddled over to the door, and turned on the outside light. "Is that snow?"

Jacob chuckled. "I think it's just sleet, but you never know."

She turned out the light, and headed toward the kitchen counter. "I'll have some coffee."

Jacob and Michelle looked at each other with raised eyebrows. Jacob said, "Do you know what to do with that?"

"Oh, Dad."

Again with the raised eyebrows, but this time they rolled their eyes and smiled.

Paradise took her coffee to the sofa and curled up by the fire.

"She can't be our little girl forever," Jacob whispered.

"Well, she is a senior, technically."

"Time flies when you're having fun." They both stared into their cups of coffee, then at each other at the same time. "We better start thinking about the future."

They watched the parade, and talked about Uncle A.J, the dolphins, and the events of the past year. Paradise kept a watch on the weather. The sleet came and went, but it melted on the ground. Jonathan and Mary arrived at eleven, and the others soon after. The house filled with laughter, jovial conversations, and the festive aroma of a feast fit for a king. Before long, the men settled in front of the television for the traditional football games, and the ladies migrated to the kitchen and dining room table.

Before the feast, Jacob was the first in a long, open, continuous prayer of thanks, in which many carried on one after another. Then they dug in.

6 A MERRY CHRISTMAS

Steve and Chelsea slowly walked back to their bungalow. "I think I can safely say that I've never had Spanish seafood for Thanksgiving, but it sure was good," Chelsea said. "Steve?"

"Yeah, me too."

"Earth to Steve, what's on your mind?"

"I'm just trying to figure it out. I mean, I know things happen for a reason, so I know why and how, but I have to figure out what to do with it."

They arrived at the bungalow. "You sit down out here. I'll make us a drink." She came back out with a couple of Rum drinks and joined him under the ceiling fan. "You want to talk about it or no?"

"The string didn't break," he said. Then silence.

"Okay?"

"When I finish a mission, the string of evidence and leads is broken. Do you understand? The only way to finish is if there are no more connections to pursue. I caught Bandweeny and he went to jail. He broke out, and I killed him. I thought the string was broken. Then came the connection to the dolphins in Nicaragua through DNA testing. The string wasn't broken."

Chelsea could see a tear in his eye, but he didn't look sad—he looked mad and determined. "I think I see where you're going with this."

"Then there was the explosion in Port A. My friends, brave men, were killed, but of course, the guys running that freighter were just the little guys at the bottom of the totem pole. Then we come here for a break, to rest and have fun, but those dolphins, and Jesse, are here. That's no coincidence. The string is alive!" He gritted his teeth, and slammed his fist against the arm of the chair.

"You're not gonna get Jesse, are you?"

"I have to get something out of him. I have to get next to him, inside of him. I have to become his friend and gain his trust."

The next morning, Steve found Robert in the maintenance shop with the mechanic.

"Ah, Steve. How are you this fine morning?"

"I was hoping we could have a little talk."

"Sure, there's coffee over there. Let me wrap up this conversation, and I'll meet you at the table outside."

Steve got a cup and went out.

Robert joined him shortly afterward. "What's on your mind?"

"It's funny how things work out."

"No doubt."

"I didn't think I'd be going back to work while we were on this little vacation, but things have changed."

"It's Jesse, isn't it?"

"The people he used to work for put a lot of people through hell, not to mention however many dolphins or other animals they exploited. People like that don't just close up shop when someone from the outside infiltrates them, they move the whole operation to a new location. I need to find that location, and Jesse may have bits and pieces of information that will point me in the right direction, if you know what I mean."

"You want to do a little covert interrogation on Jesse."

"You got it. As far as you know, does he have any idea who I am?"

"I don't think he has the faintest clue, and he probably cares even less. I've never really tried to push him, but he seems like a tough nut to crack. He stays to himself. I don't know if he has befriended anyone on the island."

"That's exactly what I wanted to hear. Only Chelsea and you know what I'm up to, can we keep it that way?"

"That's okay by me, but I think you should let Alley know because she comes into contact with everyone in the sanctuary sooner or later. It's her responsibility to know what's going on around here. She can't help you if she doesn't know what you're doing."

"I'll do that. Thanks, Robert."

"No problem. Let me know if there's anything I can do to help."

So, Steve did talk with alley to get an idea of Jesse's schedule and daily routines. He wanted to arrange his own activities so that each day he could inconspicuously cross Jesse's path. He spoke Spanish fluently, so striking up a conversation was no problem on his part. All he had to do was gain Jesse's trust.

"Steve, Jesse is a passive fellow and a bit introverted," Alley said. "I don't think he poses a threat to anyone, including the dolphins."

"I'm not after him. I have nothing against him. The only thing I'm interested in is finding out whom he may have met while he was taking care of those dolphins in Nicaragua. My ultimate goal is to find out where those people are."

"Just remember, Steve, the sanctuary is here for the animals—always protect that ideal. Angels watch over this place."

"You don't have to worry about that. I'll be patient and discrete."

"Well, he's scheduled to go out to seine fish in a little while. I can assign you to help as a volunteer."

"That's perfect, Alley." He gave her a peck on the cheek.

"I'll call you on the radio in about an hour. He and Robert should be getting the boat ready, now."

ᔕ•ᔐ

Steve found Chelsea sitting on the dock with George, Gracie, and Angela. "How are they doing?" he asked.

"They look like they're the happiest dolphins in the world," Chelsea said. "We were just talking about what kind of life these two have had, where they've been, and the people they've seen. Yet, it seems like they don't have any worries."

"Do you think they understand all that?"

"Absolutely! They certainly have the cognitive power to retain memory."

Gracie came over and eyeballed Steve. Then she mouthed the water with her mandible and let out a gentle whistle.

Steve smiled and bent over to touch her chin. "I think your right—they seem to be grateful, humble."

"I've seen a lot of dolphins come here that we know were exploited in some way, even abused, but it doesn't take long for them to put the past behind them and realize that not all humans are bad. They can see our countenance," Angela said.

"I think they're better at that than we are," Chelsea said. "They have a great capacity to judge our character, even to forgive."

"We could all learn a lesson from that, huh," Steve said.

The two girls smiled and nodded.

"What have you been doing this morning?" Chelsea asked.

"Oh, I just wondered around for a while, spoke to Robert, then ran into Alley and talked with her for a while. She said I can go out with Jesse this morning to get some fish for these guys."

"Okay, that'll be a good thing for you to do, to go out there and ride around in that clear, blue water."

"Yeah, I don't know anything about him, though. Angela, is

there anything you can tell me about him?"

"Well, just that he's a nice guy, kind of a loner. He does love dolphins. He helped us rescue a dozen dolphins from Nicaragua and stayed here to tend to them until they were released, and then he stayed on as one of our team."

"That's about all I know too."

"He doesn't speak English very well. How's your Spanish?"

"Second language."

"Then you shouldn't have any problems. He usually goes that way, around the point. There's some nice shallows over there."

They sat and watched the dolphins milling about, doing what dolphins do. Then his radio beeped. "Steve."

"Go ahead, Alley."

"If you want to head this way, he's about ready to go."

"Be there shortly." He gave Chelsea a kiss. "See you later."

ↄo•ᴏ

At four o'clock, Steve and Jesse approached the pier along side of the dolphin holding pen. They were laughing and singing a Spanish song, slapping each other on the back, and acting as if they had been friends for life.

Chelsea, Alley, Robert, Angela, and Rafael waited for their arrival. They all looked at each other with raised eyebrows and heads askant.

"Jesse always takes an ice chest full of beer," Robert said.

"I've never seen Jesse that happy," Rafael said.

Jesse pulled up to the pier, starboard side, and Rafael tied it off.

"Ah, a welcoming committee," Steve said. "We're full of fish!" The two laughed and high-fived, as they stumbled off the boat.

"You're full of something," Chelsea said with a smile and a hug.

"Hey, we got fish for the dolphins and us, and we had some fun in the meantime. Have I got a story for you."

"Well, you can tell me later. Come on, big boy, let's go home." They walked arm in arm off the pier and disappeared in the vegetation.

Steve took a shower and put on some clean clothes. Chelsea cut up some fruit and cheese, made some fruit drinks, and waited for him on the front porch.

"It looks like you broke the ice," Chelsea said.

"I did more than that, I got the whole story. It was easy. He just needed a friend to ask the right questions. We had a great afternoon. Let me start with this."

"I'm listening."

"We didn't say much until we rounded the point at the end if the island, then everything changed. It's beautiful over there. I have to take you over there. The water is so clear and shallow for about half a mile out.

"He anchored the boat in two feet of water, and as soon as we jumped out of the boat, we were surrounded by thirteen dolphins."

"Wow, I bet you didn't expect that."

"No, but better than that, he told me they were the twelve from Nicaragua, plus a baby."

"Oh, man!"

"Yeah. That's their regular meeting place. We just drank a beer and walked around in the water, in the company of dolphins that chirped, and whistled, and swam around us, rubbing against our legs."

"Fantastic." Chelsea sat on the edge of her chair, listening to his story.

"It was like a switch was flipped—he let his guard down and became a different person than everyone has described. He talked to those dolphins the same way people have a conversation. It was amazing. We had another beer, but when we pulled the net out of the boat, the dolphins disappeared."

"I guess something about the net frightened them," Chelsea said with raised eyebrows.

"That's what I thought, but he said to just wait and watch. We got another beer, and about thirty minutes later, he nodded toward the open sea. The dolphins were way out there, porpoising and swirling around, headed our way."

"Oh, I get it!"

"We finished the beers, opened the net, and just waited. It didn't take long. Those dolphins herded a school of fish right into our net. We didn't even have to move."

"Oh my God!" Chelsea laughed, and clapped, and jumped to her feet with excitement. "I knew it! I knew it!"

"Those dolphins love that man, and I could see why—they're like his family. It turns out that he has no family. The Sandinitas killed them all during the revolution. That's where we made a connection because I know the subject."

"Ah."

"It didn't take long to fill the live-well, and then we just talked and drank, and watched the dolphins."

"So you found out what you wanted to find out?"

"I didn't push him, but eventually, we got around to the story about the dolphins and the people in that racket. When I mentioned the name, Bandweeny, his eyes lit up, and I could tell he got a little flustered. Then when I said that I killed him, he started to cry, shook my hand, and hugged me like a bear."

"You went all the way!"

"The time was right. Everything just fell into place."

"So, did you get any names and places?"

"Well, we were getting into the better part of a case of beer by then. He spewed out a few names and places, but it won't take long to get all the information I need to get started."

"You're going back to work."

"How can I not, Chelsea? Look at what those bastards did to my friends, American Marines, and Port Aransas. Not to mention what they were doing with dolphins. I have to find each and every one of 'em, and put an end to it."

She sighed, and said, "I know. I know."

Christmas was fast approaching. Steve called Jacob. "Hey, cowboy."

"Steve. Have you conquered the island yet?"

"Yeah," he said with a chuckle. "Are you still planning to come for Christmas?"

"Are you kidding? You should hear my girls go on and on about it."

"Well Listen, we've made plans for ya. I talked with my pilot, Joe. He'll pick y'all up in Corpus, in my plane, and bring ya here. And when we're all ready, we'll leave together. How's that sound?"

"It sounds like we just made a deal."

"I'll give you Joe's number in Houston. He's expecting your call. Y'all decide when and let me know."

"That'll work. So, are you rested, relaxed, and recovered?"

"Couldn't be better, getting stronger every day."

"Okay. I can't wait to see the place, myself. I'll get back to you." He hung up, and went into the office. "That was Steve."

"Is everything okay?" Michelle said.

"Oh yeah, but guess what."

"What?"

"We have a free ride to Saint Croix, in his plane."

"You're kidding. That's wonderful."

"And then, we'll all come back home together."

"That's great. I was just looking at airlines. I can't wait to tell Paradise."

"Well, now we know how we're going, we just have to figure out when. I need to call his pilot, Joe, and finalize the plans."

"We'll find out Paradise's holiday schedule at school, tonight, then you can call Joe."

"Sounds like a plan."

At dinner, Paradise had some questions. "I can't figure out if it's a sad thing or a good thing that there has to be places of sanctuary in the world for animals. On the one hand, it says that the world is such an unsafe place for animals to live that we have to provide special protection for them. On the other hand, it says that humanity is compassionate and willing to provide that extra protection for those that need it."

Jacob and Michelle looked at each other, and Michelle took the first run at it. "It's a good question. It exercises critical thinking. I prefer to think of it in terms of the latter. God loves His animals, and He called for us to be stewards of the earth. It is inevitable that some animals and humans are going to need extra protection at some point in their lives. At the same time, He has called a select few to provide that protection, and He takes care of them. It is a good thing."

"Dad?"

"Well, darlin, I tend to think of it in terms of the former. There are more bad people in the world than good people. Bad people do bad things. We experienced that first-hand with Bandweeny and Destiny. Bad people are driven by money, and the exploitation of animals is big money. Everything we've been doing in the recent past was to correct the wrongs done by bad people to God's animals. Because of bad people, animals, even some humans, need a place of sanctuary. It is a sad thing."

There was silence around the table. Paradise stared at her food with crunched eyebrows, then up at her mom and dad, and said, "But y'all didn't answer my question, you simply expressed each side."

"That's because you posed a philosophical question," Michelle said. "To which the only answer for you must be your own conclusion in the matter. You have to make up your own mind. We can't tell you how to think."

ഗ•ഛ

On December twenty first, The Andersons loaded their things in the van, said their good-byes to Greg, Amber, and the dolphins, and made their way to the Corpus Christi Airport to meet Joe. They were headed to Saint Croix for Christmas.

"Jacob, you want to join me up front in the co-pilot's seat?" Joe asked.

"You bet, but I know nothing about flying."

"Then don't touch anything." They both chuckled. "I will show you some basic controls and instrument, just in case I keel over at thirty thousand feet."

Joe started the two jet engines, gave Jacob a headset, and went through the preflight checklist. "This is a state of the arts private jet. It could practically make the flight by itself, even land, if it had to. I can talk to you and the ground. You can only talk to me. If you need to talk to the ground just flip that switch."

When it was time to go, he called back to the girls, "Are y'all strapped in and ready to go?"

"Yes," Michelle answered.

He spoke to the tower, pushed the throttle forward, and taxied to the runway. "Here we go." With a gentle lurch, the plane sped down the runway until it rose from the earth and climbed toward the heavens.

"How long will it take?" Paradise asked.

"It's eighteen hundred and seventy-five miles at five hundred miles an hour, so we'll be there in about four hours," Joe answered. "But, you have to remember that they are two hours ahead of us, so on the clock, it'll look like it took six hours."

By the time wheels touched down on the Island of Saint Croix, the spirit of Christmas had Paradise worked into an energized state of mind. Not only was she going to see Steve and Chelsea, but George, Gracie, Alley, and Robert as well. This was her first time out of the United States, and her first time to a tropical island.

Her mind kept going back to the time when the angel, Lucas, gave her the card with Alley's phone number, and told her to call it. She thought, *this must be part of my destiny that God would show me how He loves and protects his animals throughout the world. Surely, this will be a blessing of knowledge and wisdom that I can keep and take with me wherever He leads me to go in life.*

Joe taxied the plane from the runway to a small hangar Steve had rented for a week. As they approached, Paradise's nose was glued to the window, taking in all the sights of a new world.

"Look, Mom, There's Steve and Chelsea!"

After the plane was tucked away in the hangar, Steve took the scenic route back to the sanctuary. "I'll give you the same tour that Robert gave us, just to give you an idea of the city."

Alley and Robert met the van at the sanctuary. "Welcome to the island," Alley said, as she gave Paradise a big hug. "I'm so glad you could come, and for Christmas, no less."

"I am too. This place is beautiful. Can we go see the dolphins?"

Alley chuckled. "Maybe we should show y'all your bungalows first, and unload your stuff. Then we'll go to the beach." And so they did.

George and Gracie were excited when they saw Paradise. They jumped, flipped, chattered, and squealed. The people clapped and laughed.

"Hi, Gracie. Hi, George," Paradise said. "It's so good to see y'all again. You look healthy and happy."

The dolphins celebrated so more.

Paradise took a three hundred and sixty degrees look around the dock. "This is a fantastic place you have here."

"Thank you, sweetie," Alley said.

"When are you going to set them free?"

"Funny you should ask. I started to last week, but God stopped me. He said that you should be the one to open the gate. I couldn't argue with that."

Paradise grinned from ear to ear, and a tear of joy trickled down her cheek, and she kind of started shaking a little bit.

Alley reached over and pulled her to her side. "It's just like at home, sweetie. You're not saying goodbye to them. You're just giving them the gift that God has always intended for them to have. Believe me, they'll come back to see ya every day you're here, and any time you come back. They will always remember and love you for opening that gate."

She looked at her mom and dad, and let out a short burst of crying compassion. By then, everyone had wet eyes, and Jacob and Michelle gave her a nod.

"Can I do it now?"

"Whenever you're ready, dear."

So Paradise walked over to the gate, and called the dolphins. They came and poised in front of her. She bent over and rubbed their rostrums. "You guys have waited a long time for this. You've endured the hardships from bad humans most of your lives, and now comes your reward, freedom. You couldn't be in a better place, or with better people. You are safe here. There are angels watching over you. You will never be imprisoned in a swimming pool again. This time, your freedom will be forever." She rubbed them again. "Y'all be good kids, okay?"

The dolphins nodded and chirped.

"Now you go out there and find some new friends to play with. Well then, are you ready?"

The dolphins nodded and chirped.

Paradise stood up, grabbed the top of the gate, and pulled it open.

In a flash, with one thrust of her tail flukes, Gracie leapt through the gate with George fast at her tail. The people clapped, cried, and laughed at the same time. The dolphins went about twenty yards from the dock, stopped and turned, chattered and nodded, then jumped twelve feet into the air. Porpoising through the water, the two dolphins made their way out into the Caribbean to begin their new adventures in life, free from the exploitation and imprisonment of mankind forever.

The next morning, Paradise was up before the sun. *I can't wait to see the sunrise over the Caribbean*, she thought. *I wonder if George and Gracie will come back like Alley said.*

She started making a pot of coffee, just as her parents were getting up.

"You're up early," Michelle said.

"I don't want to miss a thing. I want to see the sunrise."

"That sounds like a good idea," Jacob said. "Why don't we all go down to the pier and see what an island sunrise is like."

So, they all grabbed a cup of coffee and a banana and headed to the beach. Jacob took his hand-radio. The moon was still up, and twilight began to break. As they cleared the tree line and stepped out onto the beach, they were awed that the moon illuminated the white sand. But that wasn't all, they saw the green glow from the bioluminescence of the dinoflagellates as the water was stirred by dolphins and other aquatic animals. They sat on the pier.

"I've seen bioluminescence before," Jacob said, "but it wasn't this widespread."

Another manly voice spoke up. "I've been out there walking on the water, communicating with the minds of the sea."

They all turned to see who was standing behind them.

"Jarrell!" Paradise said.

"Hello, Paradise. Father is pleased that you took his advice. What do you think of our sanctuary?"

"I love it. It's more beautiful than I expected." Then they heard the chirping of dolphins. "They did come back, Mom, just like Alley said."

"And brought some new friends with them," Michelle said.

"If you will go out in the boat today, you will see the representation of animals that thrive here. I'm sure you will be amazed at the variety," Jarrell said. "And tomorrow, ask Alley to give you a tour of the forest, and you will be amazed again."

"Jarrell, this is my Mom and Dad."

"Yes, we've met. I'm sorry I had to stun you the first time we met, but Destiny had to be born, and Father couldn't allow anyone to interfere with my mission to make that happen. I'm sure you understand."

"Oh, absolutely! No problem," Jacob said.

"He is very happy with all the work y'all have done with His animals, but there is more to do. In the near future, you will take Paradise around the world to visit other sanctuaries and places where dolphins are abused. Your life's work will become apparent and you will know it without a doubt. Enjoy your visit here. Everything is well at home. Farewell for now." And he disappeared.

They all sat quietly for a minute.

"That's awesome!" Jacob said. "Everything we do has a meaning and a purpose. We all got up at the same time, came down here together, and an angel waited for us. Awesome!"

"I still have goose bumps," Michelle said.

"Me to."

They sat quietly watching the dolphins milling around the pier, doing what dolphins do. As the sun peeked over the horizon, Jacob's radio beeped.

"Are y'all down at the pier?" Alley said.

"Yeah."

"I thought you might be. How 'bout some breakfast?"

"That sounds good. We'll see ya in a minute."

ৎ৯•ঙ২

Steve convinced Jesse to take Chelsea and the Andersons on a boat tour around the island, especially to meet the thirteen dolphins at the point.

"Not only will you enjoy it," Steve told his friends, "but when he sees how much y'all know and love dolphins, he may open up some more and speak freely about the smuggling operation."

So they loaded the boat with food and drinks, and headed out for a day of fun and adventure on the Caribbean. The Americans in the boat could speak a little Spanish, but not the same dialect as Jesse, so Steve acted as translator when needed.

At the point, they played with the thirteen dolphins, and Jesse quickly learned that Paradise was a dolphin whisperer.

She pointed and said, "That girl is pregnant."

"How do you know?" Jesse asked.

"She told me."

Jesse looked at Steve, with his head askant.

Steve just nodded.

"What else does she say?" Jesse asked.

"They are all very grateful to you. They know that you are the one that rescued them. They thought they would die in that little pen. You were the only one that came to them, talked to them, and fed them. They love you."

He dropped his head, squinched his face, and a single tear trickled down his cheek. "Can you tell them things?"

"I can, but they already know."

He smiled, reaching down to pet one of the dolphins. At that moment, Jesse became a friend to the Andersons and Chelsea.

Jesse told Michelle to ready her telephoto lens and for everyone to get ready for a show. "If you really want to see a show, we'll go out there where the whales live, and you'll never forget this day as long as you live."

So, they got back in the boat and headed out to sea. "You will see dolphins and whales that seem to be out of place, but they're quite at home here. I still can't tell you what three quarters of them are, but I'm learning."

After about three miles, he pulled back on the throttle and pointed.

Michelle looked through her telephoto. "Jacob, that looks like a pod of striped dolphins!"

As if on cue, binoculars and cameras came out, and shutters started clicking.

"We'll get closer," Jesse said. "This is the only boat they see in the sanctuary, all other boats are prohibited without permit."

"How is that regulated," Chelsea asked.

"Since this is the U.S. Virgin Islands, the American Coast Guard patrols the sea, especially the borders of the sanctuary."

"Where are the borders?"

Jesse pulled up a map on his GPS and zoomed out. He slowed the boat and put it in neutral so everyone could see and hear what he said, "These are electronic buoys. They send an alert warning to any GPS within twenty-five miles, and they're on all the nautical navigation charts."

"It's huge!" Paradise said. "I had no idea it was so big."

"You'll see why soon enough." So, he resumed his path out to sea at a slower pace, pointing as he went mile after mile into the Caribbean.

They saw common dolphins, spotted dolphins, dusky dolphins, spinner dolphins, and many more.

"What's that, Mom?"

"That looks like a Risso's dolphin. Jacob, is that a pair of Frazier's dolphins?"

"Yes it is! Aren't they beautiful? Paradise, this is the best classroom you could have."

"Dad, what's that? It doesn't have a dorsal fin."

"That's a southern right whale dolphin. That's only the second one I've seen. A white beak and ventral side, black on top. There's Atlantic white-sided dolphins."

"I saw something blow over there," Chelsea said. "It's a false killer whale."

As the boat moved further out to sea, the pelagic Cetaceans became more abundant, and while the whale watchers watched, Steve scooted closer to Jesse and asked some questions. "I've been thinking about our friends from Nicaragua, have you remembered anything else you might have seen or heard?"

Jesse scratched his head and paused. "They used to ask me to pick up postal parcels for them, on my way to the dolphins. They came from many places in the world, but one more than any other—Caracas. The parcels from there had the same insignias as the guys that paid me."

Steve leaned back and raised his eyebrows, then leaned forward to Jesse. "Can you describe that insignia?"

"It was a red dragon, standing on its hind legs, breathing fire. It held a shield in its left forepaw, and a spear in the right. The spearhead was covered and dripping with blood."

Steve smiled and slapped Jesse on the back, then slid back to Chelsea's side.

"Dad!" Paradise said with excitement.

"Oh my gosh. That's a mother and pup sperm whale. Man, there's no telling what we're gonna see out here, today."

They stayed out all day and made it back to the boathouse at dusk.

"I'm ready for some dinner, how about y'all?" Jacob said. So, the whole gang headed for the mess hall, except Steve.

"Chelsea, bring me back something, anything. I have some homework to do."

Ꙥ•ҩ

Steve went to their bungalow and made a phone call to his contact in the CIA. "Fred, Steve."

"Hey, buddy, back from the dead, huh?"

"Yeah, don't spread that around too far. I need some research help."

"Name it."

"I'm after the people that sent those two freighters to Texas, and killed my men. I'm looking for an insignia. An informant tells me it's a red dragon, standing on its hind legs, breathing fire. It's holding a shield in its left forepaw, and a spear in its right. The spearhead is covered and dripping with blood."

"That should be easy enough to find. I'll get back to ya."

He went inside, poured a glass of wine, got a cigar and his

laptop, and went back to the front porch. He pulled up a map of Caracas, Venezuela and began to study it.

His phone rang. "Yeah."

"That was easy. It's one of the biggest organized crime rings in the world—Chinese. They have affiliates on every continent, except Antarctica. I'm sending you a file right now."

"Thanks, buddy. I owe ya one."

"Come see me next time you're out this way."

"Will do. Later."

His computer beeped. He opened the file with anticipation. *They're certainly not trying to hide*, he thought. *Even arrogant in their advertising—perhaps, pride will be their downfall.*

He studied the file meticulously until he found the connection to Nicaragua. He traced their connections, and putting two and two together, he located the operation in Caracas. After a brief moment of thought, he closed the laptop and ran down the steps, just as the rest of the gang approached from the mess hall. "I'll be right back. I have to talk to Jesse." And he disappeared in the jungle.

A few minutes later, he arrived at Jesse's bungalow. "I want to show you something." He opened his laptop.

Jesse was startled. "That's it. That's the dragon."

Then Steve scrolled to the next picture. "Do you recognize him?"

"That's Manuel!"

"Who's he?"

"Manuel Gomez was the boss man in Nicaragua."

"Okay, look at this." He showed Jesse a map of Caracas. "I'm sure that is the operation in Caracas, but I need to go there and put my eyes on it to verify that. My plane is at the airport. Will you go with me tomorrow? All I want to do is watch the place for a little while and try to identify anyone that comes and goes."

"You'll catch them and punish them?"

"Eventually! That's the plan."

"I'll go."

"Thank you. We'll leave at five in the morning. We'll come back tomorrow."

The he went over to Joe's bungalow. "Do you have plans for tomorrow?"

"Not that I know of."

"Good. I want you to fly Jesse and me over to Caracas at five in the morning." And he showed him the evidence and told him the plan. "Call the airport and have them ready the plane."

ა•ა

It was two days before Christmas. Steve, Jesse, and Joe took off from Saint Croix, headed for Caracas, Venezuela.

"Give it the gas, Joe. I don't want this to take all day."

"Aye-aye, Captain," Joe replied, and shoved the throttle forward.

"I arranged for our man in Caracas to meet us at the airport with a car. He doesn't know it yet, but I'm gonna recruit him for surveillance. Jesse and I will go with him for a couple of hours. You stay with the plane. Okay, buddy?"

Joe just nodded.

Steve went back to the cabin with Jesse, opened his laptop, and studied the CIA file. He went over the plan of the day with Jesse. "I've got a local man meeting us at the airport with a car. He's gonna take us where we need to go. I just need for you to watch and listen, but if you see or think of anything important, speak up. We're gonna take you where we think Gomez might be. If you see him, let us know, or anyone else you might recognize."

Jesse just nodded.

It wasn't long before Joe called out. "I've got clearance. We're starting descent . . . about fifteen minutes."

Steve got everything ready, and they buckled up for the landing. The wheels touched down, and Joe taxied to the appointed waiting area at the Simón Bolivar International Airport of Maiquetia, La Guaira, Venezuela.

As Steve opened the door of the plane and lowered the steps, a man got out of a car and approached the plane. Steve went down to meet him. "It's a great day."

"Not if you're a dragon" the man replied. They shook hands.

"Steve Bly."

"Alfonzo Martinez. Just call me, Fonzie."

"Come on in, we'll talk about it."

They all sat around the table in the plane's cabin. Steve opened his laptop and began to show Fonzie the file.

"I know this organization, we call them *The Bloody Dragon*," Fonzie said. "They've been on our radar for years. They have an outpost on every continent, except Antarctica."

Then Steve got to the pictures of Manuel Gomez.

"I've seen alerts about this man, but I haven't seen him."

"That's who we're looking for. Jesse did some work for him in Nicaragua, taking care of smuggled dolphins. Last year, I captured a man, Aston Kaiser, from Gomez's operation in Nicaragua for trafficking dolphins from the U.S. He's in our prison right now. But, Gomez got pissed off, moved his operation here, and tried to blow up Texas. He killed some of my Marines, and I spent three months in a hospital. I want him."

"What are you going to do with him?"

"God only knows." He smiled and winked.

"I have the perfect place to start—*The Bloody Dragon* headquarters. It's about twelve miles from here."

"Let's go."

Steve, Jesse, and Fonzie exited the plane, got in the car, and left the airport. Fonzie went west on Highway L-06. After about fifteen minutes, he turned into a parking lot of a large warehouse district used for shipping and commerce in and out of Caracas.

"This whole area that we've been driving in, including the airport, is known as the Federal District. The National Police do not bother any illegal operations here as long as they get kickbacks."

He drove through the rows of warehouses until he came to a stop. He handed Steve a pair of binoculars and pointed. "Isn't it obvious?"

Steve peered through the glasses for a moment. "Well, they're not afraid to advertise, are they."

"Like I said."

"Let's find a good spot to sit and watch."

ॐ•ॐ

On Christmas Eve, the whole gang went into town to capture the Christmas spirit—island style.

"You're lucky," Robert said. "With winter only three days old, it stands to reason that our first cold front would arrive today. It's a balmy sixty-five. It must be really cold up your way."

"Does it get colder than this?" Jacob asked.

Maybe a few degrees, but our average low is about seventy-one."

They strolled through the retail district, and had lunch at a well-visited bistro.

That evening, Alley invited The Andersons, Chelsea, and Steve to her house for an early Christmas dinner.

"Hi y'all, come on in," Alley said. "On Christmas Day, you'll find that the feast in the mess hall will be continental. I just wanted to share a more traditional dinner with you. So, we have turkey, ham, and all the trimmings that we Americans are use to."

"Thank you, Alley. You're so sweet," Michelle said.

"Plus, I have something to give Paradise."

Paradise perked up. "Oh, I wonder what it is."

So, the girls helped Alley prepare the table while guys watched part of the football bowl game that was on television, and enjoyed some Brandy and cigars.

"How'd it go, yesterday?" Jacob asked Steve. "Can you talk about it?"

"Very well, we found the son of a bitch."

"Did you give him a piece of led for Christmas?"

"Nah, he won't get off that easy. I've got plans for that one. I've got eyes and ears on him, while I train a team for a specific mission. It won't take too long. We'll get him." He smiled, winked, and took a drink.

Jacob and Robert smiled, and the glasses clinked.

After the main courses were replaced with pies, cakes, and other assorted desserts, the guys went back to the television.

"Follow me, girls," Alley said. She led them down the hallway to her office. On a tabletop sat a small pile of paperwork. "This is for you, Paradise. Go ahead, take a look."

Paradise started at the top with a folder full of photographs.

"I took those from space, in the shuttle, Columbia. Those are the spots with the green glow in the water that caught my eye. That first one is this place."

"This is awesome!" she gave Alley a hug, and her eyes began to water. "I couldn't ask for anything better than this. You know why the water is so bright at night?"

"The phytoplankton."

Paradise giggled. "Well, that too, but the angels are out there, walking on the water, playing with the whales and dolphins— tending to their needs . . ."

"And that stirs up the water. I hadn't thought of that." And she smiled.

"She didn't either," Michelle said. "Jarrell told us yesterday morning on the pier." And all the girls laughed.

The girls were enthralled with the pictures, enhanced by the comments of the astronaut that took them.

"This is a world map marking all the spots in those pictures.

These are all marine sanctuaries, globally recognized, but not all are publicly announced."

"This is amazing!" Michelle said. "I had no idea."

"This is a catalog of all the sanctuaries with a Table of Contents."

"Wow! You put all this together for me?" Paradise asked.

"I did, but I had a little help. I got the idea on the flight back with George and Gracie. Before y'all came, I gathered all the information from my shelves, took it to the Kinko's in town, and they made copies and compiled the catalog for me. You're gonna need this information in the future."

ఇ•ఎ

Each Christmas on the island, Alley and Robert procured a small tree for all the crew and guests. So, during the night, Jacob and Michelle wrapped the gifts they bought while on the island, and together with those they brought from home, placed them under the tree.

Christmas morning was much like at home, without the winter affect. Michelle was up first, making coffee and pancakes. Jacob woke to the aroma. Paradise soon followed. As usual, it was a quiet, calm, and lazy morning. And, after the typical practices of the event, Paradise went down to the beach to see if George and

Gracie were there.

Sure enough, they were. So, she sat on dock and talked to them for a while. "This may be the last time I see you guys for a while. We're going back home in the morning."

The dolphins nodded and chirped.

"I won't worry about you because I know you are happy and taken care of here, but I will miss you."

Gracie swam in a tight circle, made a shallow breach, and returned to Paradise.

"Merry Christmas, Paradise."

She looked up to see Jarrell.

He sat beside her. "Have you enjoyed your trip to sanctuary?"

She started crying and gave him a hug.

"Now, now." He patted her on the back. "I know your emotions are enriched. It's never easy to say by to loved ones, but then, you know this isn't really, good bye."

She smiled, chuckled, and sat upright. "I know. These flesh bodies are so uncontrollable sometimes. I've had a wonderful time here. Thank you."

"Don't thank me, thank our Father. He planned it all out for you. Do you now have a better picture of your future?"

"I've been thinking about that, and I think I'm beginning to understand. Can I ask you a question?"

"Anything."

"What do you do in Heaven on Christmas Day?"

He laughed. "Ah, well, in Paradise, as we call it, on the right side of the gulf there is a day-long celebration of the day that Yeshua was conceived in Mary's womb. On the left side of the gulf there is continued despair, wailing, and gnashing of teeth."

"Wow, you answered me straight."

"Have I ever done differently?"

"No."

"Well then, if you are okay now, I will leave you with your friends, and return to the celebration. I'll see you at home, next time. Christ in you, Paradise Anderson." And he vanished into thin air.

The next morning was a busy one. They gathered and pack their belongings, loaded the van, and said their good byes. Steve went to say farewell to Jesse.

At the airport, as the luggage was loaded into the plane, Steve paid his bill for storage and maintenance of the plane. It was time to go home. There were handshakes, hugs, and tears.

"Thank you, Alley," Paradise said. "I am fortunate to have a friend like you."

"It is I that is privileged to have you in my life, little dear one."

Alley and Robert waved as the plane taxied to the runway.

7 RINGS

It was their first morning at home after the trip to Saint Croix for Christmas. Jacob was outside, checking the property. Michelle was in the kitchen.

Jacob came in through the back door. "Brr! It's cold out there. If I didn't know better, I'd say it was about to snow. Is that biscuits and gravy and sausage?"

"Yes it is."

"Oh, you wonderful wife, you," and he gave her a big hug and a kiss.

"It's nice to go away for a while, but it's even better to come home. I thought you'd like this."

"You know me so well, Michelle."

"How's everything out there? Are the kiddies here?"

"Yeah, they're all huddled up under the edge of the dock. I think they like the cold for a change, just like we do."

"Well, they are Texans. Did you talk to Greg last night?"

"Yeah, he'll be here for lunch. It sure is nice to have a couple of good friends like Jonathan and him. He took care of everything around here the same, as I would have. It's like we never left."

"I know. He left me little messages around the house, that he checked this or that, and everything was okay." She handed him a cup of coffee. "Speaking of Jonathan, they're coming for lunch too. I'm uploading the island pictures onto a flash drive. I'll just run a slideshow on the TV."

"Good idea, and some background Christmas music."

"Yeah."

"I'm gonna start a fire. What else smells so good?"

"I just put some pumpkin pies in the oven. I figured I'd make some salad, and order some pizzas. How does that sound?"

"I like it." He turned on the local morning news. "Michelle."

"What?"

"He just said it's lightly snowing over in Sinton."

"Nice. Maybe we'll get lucky again—so much for *global warming*. I'm gonna call Chelsea."

"Ah, leave em along, Michelle."

She threw a biscuit at him.

Chelsea answered the phone. "Hello."

"How's everything over there?"

"First cup of coffee—he's on the phone with Washington. He mumbled something about the Governor, DOJ, DOD, NSA, and CIA. Then he picked up his phone. He's been on it for almost an hour."

꽁•꽂

Paradise faced her final semester in high school. Her formative years of youth were shaped and molded by Michelle and home schooling, though she came to love her new friends and teachers in public high school. She waddled into the kitchen—yawned, stretched, and laid her head on Michelle's shoulder. "That was a good sleep, but I woke up dreaming I was taking a test at school."

"Are you ready to buckle down and graduate this semester?" Michelle asked.

"Yeah, but it's kind of sad, though."

"How do you mean?"

"Well, knowing that school is coming to an end. I've been going to school for so long—it's all I know how to do, for the most part."

"Don't forget about college."

"That's what I'm talking about, Mom, it's frightening. Everything will change. My whole life will change."

Michelle laughed. "Ah, the rings. You're beginning to see them. You just don't know what they are yet. You'll learn. That doesn't have to be a bad thing. Don't forget that you're not the only girl in the world that graduated high school and went to college."

"But Mom, look at Terry—he went to Austin and virtually disappeared from my life, and some of the stories he tells are horrible. I mean, the professors are all liberals, and they try to brainwash him to be what they want him to be, rather than allowing him to become what he wants to become."

"Paradise, it doesn't have to be that way for everyone. You have a strong background. You have a strong personality. You have a strong foundation in life to build on. You have already lived through experiences in life that challenged your ability to overcome. And you persevered. I know it all seems so overwhelming at first, but that is what life is made of. Life is full of challenges and choices that require your own judgement in each individual matter that arises. We all learn how to live life by accepting challenges, meeting them head-on, and coming out on the other side, successful. That is what builds our character. You already know this."

"Well, yeah, but . . .."

"But, nothing! I'm confident that your Dad and I have raised you up to be able to face any situation that life can throw at you and you can handle it. Don't be a 'pity baby.' There's nothing in the world that can happen to you that hasn't happened to other people somewhere in time throughout the history of mankind—and you have God on your side. Now I'll ask you again, are you ready to finish this semester and graduate?"

"Yes, ma'am!"

"That's better."

ഗ⦁ഩ

Steve was obsessed. He couldn't believe how easy it was to find the man that ordered two freighters, full of explosives, to Texas, but there he was. *I can't let him get away with it*, he thought. *I'm the best man for the job, and there's no better time than the present.* He made another call.

"I hear what you're saying, Steve," said the Secretary of

National Security. "I'm not arguing with you. You know how this works, you give me a plan, and I'll present it to the White House for approval."

"Thank you, Sir. I'll get back to you."

The next call he made was to the same group of former Navy SEALs that help him get Bandweeny, on the southern gulf coast of Mexico, to arrange a meeting. Then he called the Director of the FBI to get information on the investigations of the two freighters that attacked Texas. He received a file from the Director in thirty minutes.

"Chelsea, I need a favor, dear. I need you to let me have your apartment for a couple of hours. I have a couple of important friends coming over from Corpus to help me devise a plan to get Gomez and his cohorts. Do you mind?"

"Not at all. I'll just go over to Michelle's. Call me when you're done, and I'll come get you."

"Thanks, babe."

Chelsea took a shower, got dressed, and when she opened the door to leave, there were two men standing there about to knock. She gasped.

"Sorry, ma'am, we didn't mean to startle you."

"That's okay. I was just on my way out. Steve, your friends are here."

Steve came to the door. "Hi, guys. This is Chelsea. That's Clint and Trevor. Come on in, guys. I'll call ya later, babe." They kissed, and she left.

"Nice girl," Clint said.

"Salt of the earth. Make yourselves at home guys. There's a pot of coffee, juice, or some good stuff if you want."

They sat at the table. "Our target is a small part of a world-wide organized crime ring that Bandweeny dealt with over the years. These particular people were based in Nicaragua until I captured one of them and some DNA samples from their lab. That pissed-off the leader, Manuel Gomez." He showed them a picture. "He retaliated by sending two freighters, full of explosives, to Texas— one to Houston and one right here to Port Aransas. That one killed four of our colleagues, and put me in the hospital for months."

"Where are they now," Trevor asked.

"Gomez moved his operation from Nicaragua to Caracas. I have seen it and him, but I don't know if that is temporary or permanent. Of course, I want to move ASAP, so we don't lose him. I have CIA eyes and ears on him now. This guy is a real thug. He makes Bandweeny look like a school child. He traffics everything—

drugs, money, electronics, guns, and people. He has tortured and executed hundreds, if not thousands, of people, including men, women, and children."

"What do you want to do with him?" Trevor asked.

"Well, I'd love to just shoot him in the head, but I'd rather work on him for a while."

"Ah, some interrogation!"

"You bet. I want to occupy an office right in his neighborhood, stir him up a little, like an ant bed. Then when they least expect it, we'll swoop in and take as many as we can get."

"Guns, darts, knives, or grenades?"

"No, we'll have fun with them later, but the first thing I want to do is ambush their security system—fix it so we can switch it to a continuous loop whenever we want."

"When do you want to go," Clint asked.

"I'm working on the office, maybe within a week."

"What then?"

"We devise a plan. I give it to the Secretary of National Security. He presents it to the White House. They approve it, and we go."

"Okay, let's hear it."

"I think the best plan is a stealth extraction. I'll get a floor plan of the building, personnel identifications, behavior movements, and routines. We'll fly down. My man will meet us at the airport with a large van. We'll do the surveillance ourselves.

"When we're ready, we'll enter the building at night, and take 'em one by one as they come in, put em to sleep, and bring 'em back to the U.S."

"I like it. It's been a while since we did a job like that. It sounds like fun," Trevor said.

"I agree," Clint said. "Let's do it!"

"Notify your team. I'll be in touch."

ॐ•ॐ

At his New Year's Eve party, Jacob cornered Steve. "I know you're planning something. I can see it in your eyes."

"You're right. I'm gonna get that son of a bitch and make him pay for what he did, and what he's been doing for a long time. His ship has sailed—he's going home."

"You gonna put his lights out?"

"I'm gonna send him to God and let Him deal with him, but

he's gonna know who sent him there." He winked.

Jacob smiled.

"I've got to go home to Houston, tomorrow, so I can put my face back on—if you know what I mean."

"I do. How you gonna get there?"

"I guess a commercial flight."

"Why don't you let me drive ya? We can talk, and I can finally see where you come from."

Steve cocked his head askant then back. "Okay. Don't drink too much, tonight."

So, on New Year's morning, Steve and Jacob left Port Aransas, bright and early, for Houston. It was cold, gray, and drizzly. They didn't go north to catch a major highway. They just hugged the Texas coast on a State Highway that made the trip a direct path into Steve's driveway. It took four and a half-hours.

✀•❧

Two days later, Jacob pulled into his own driveway.

Michelle met him at the door with a hug and kiss. "How was the drive? Did you enjoy that?"

"Man, that was great. I forgot how good it feels to drive across

Texas. I almost felt guilty for having so much fun."

"I knew you'd be ready for lunch when you got back, so I have some homemade hamburgers ready to cook if you want."

"Yeah, that sounds good."

"So tell me . . . what is Steve's private life like."

"Well, let me see, how can I say it? He certainly has all the elements of a playboy's lifestyle, but I think he maintains a disciplined, subdued kind of life."

"Really?"

"Yeah. He has a large, beautiful townhouse with a golf course for a back yard. He has a nice fishing boat in a slip at a marina just a few blocks from his house. And, his office is just around the corner from Johnson Space Center."

"That sure sounds like a playboy."

"Except for the fact that he has no golf clubs, no fishing poles, and he's not an astronaut. So, go figure."

"Well, is it still a mystery? I mean. Didn't we always think of him as a playboy?"

"I still can't say one way or the other. He may have some clubs in a locker at the pro shop. He may have fishing poles in a storage bin on the boat. He certainly knows some astronauts—I met a few, but he talked a lot about his clients and guests. Maybe those perks are more for them than him. I don't know."

ক•ও

Steve got regular updates on The Bloody Dragon in Caracas from Fonzie. "I've seen several shipments come and go since you were here. One of them was a dozen young girls. They were all tied together. The guys handling them shuffled them from a truck to the building and back. Then the truck left."

"What kind of shape were the girls in?"

"They didn't look good, Steve. They looked tired, worn out. Their clothes were ragged, their hair all messed up. Looked like they hadn't had a good meal or a bath in a long time. There was nothing I could do but watch."

"They're gonna pay for that, Fonzie. We're gonna get them. Are there any new faces showing up?"

"Yeah. I've identified the headman of the operation, Zhang Li. He looks like a mean son of a bitch, and a bodyguard follows him around."

"You're taking pictures of all this, right?"

"Yeah."

"Send them to me. Is everything okay with the new office?"

"Yeah. I spend a lot of time here. I don't want to be seen going in and out too much. We're across the row, a couple of doors down. Perfect location."

"So, how many men hang around there during the day?"

"Well, except for the truck drivers and laborers that are random, I've counted fifteen regulars. Two of them come in at seven A.M. The others start streaming in here after that. But Steve, there's a whole company of men over at the shipyards. They come and go throughout the day, and the place is empty by sundown."

"Thanks, Fonzie. I think we'll be there next week. I'll let you know." As soon as he hung up the phone, it rang. "Hello."

"Steve Bly?"

"Who's calling?"

"This is FBI Special Agent, Isaiah Stenson."

"Do you know who I am, Isaiah?"

"Yes, Sir. I had to check your credentials before I made this call. It's an honor to speak to you, Sir."

"Go ahead, Isaiah. What's on your mind?"

"Sir, a mutual friend told me you were seeking information about the terrorist's attack in Port Aransas, Texas. I have some new information that you might find helpful."

"Thank you, go ahead."

"Sir, each of the two ships that invaded Texas came directly from Caracas, Venezuela. They were both retired freighters, slated to voyage to the ship graveyards in Alang, India. When they left port, They headed directly for Texas instead."

"Do you have any evidence that the Venezuelan Government had any involvement?"

"Not directly. All we know is that they made no effort to stop the ships."

"So, as far as you know, this was a private operation."

"Yes, Sir."

"Do you have any information regarding the explosives recovered from the Houston ship?"

"Yes, Sir. Our forensics lab has determined that they were Chinese munitions."

"Hmm! Were they dirty?"

"No, Sir. They had the capability, but not the material."

"Anything else, Isaiah?"

"Yes, Sir. I did some digging into past records and found that those particular munitions were never transferred from the Chinese Government to the Venezuelan Government, but one name kept popping up—a Chinese organization called, The Bloody Dragon."

It wasn't hard to figure out—that phone call confirmed all of his suspicions. Moreover, he knew that the CIA and the FBI had two sets of information, and he was in the middle of both, which was exactly where he wanted to be. He invited his closest friend and partner to his house to discuss the whole thing from top to bottom.

"So, what do you think, Joe? Can you think of one piece of information that I don't have, but need?"

"Well, the only thing you haven't mentioned is what we're going to do with them once we have them."

Steve dropped his head and gently nodded. Then rubbed his chin as though he was in deep thought. "I still haven't made my mind up on that one. You know I've always followed the law, but these guys have really rubbed me the wrong way. I want them to suffer."

"Do you want my opinion?"

"That's why you're here, Joe."

"Before we even load them in the truck, we make them deaf, dumb, and blind—sedative, blindfold, ear plugs, and tape their mouths. We bring them back here to the hangar and play with them for a couple of days before we call the marshals. But, that Gomez dude, we know everything about him that we need. The Gulf of Mexico is very big, and very deep, if you know what I mean. A lot of things can happen at thirty thousand feet."

Steve smiled, winked, and didn't say a word, as he got two glasses and poured some Jack Daniels. They toasted and took a drink.

He scrolled his computer to his proposal. In the "subject" line he typed, "EXPEDITE!" and hit, "SEND."

ം•ം

Steve and Joe loaded their gear in the plane's cargo hold.

"Clothes, armor, night vision, communications" Joe went through the checklist. "Medical, gas masks, gas canisters, electronics, miscellaneous hardware, arsenal, and food and water provisions. We've got it all, Steve."

Steve walked over to a shelf, picked up a heavy burlap sack, and took it to the plane.

"Uh, we don't have a chain on the list, Steve."

"You never know when we might need to tie something up." He tossed it in the plane.

Steve shut down the office, while Joe warmed up the plane and backed it out of the hangar. Then Steve turned the key to close the hangar doors, got in the plane, pulled up the steps, and secured the hatch. He sat in the co-pilot's seat and took out his phone. "Clint, we're on our way."

Joe taxied to the runway and they took off for Corpus Christi. It was a short flight. They landed forty-five minutes later. Clint, Trevor, Vic, and Zack were ready to go. Joe didn't even shut down the plane. They loaded their gear, and took off for Caracas.

"We're going to have some fun, guys. We're going to take some real assholes out of commission, just sit back, and enjoy the ride," Steve said. Then he pushed a button, and a slideshow of their mission played on the forward screen. There were pictures of the airport, the route to the target location, maps, satellite images, and pictures of the key characters involved. Steve's preparation was very thorough.

�����

Gomez walked through the warehouse to the back loading dock and spoke to his first mate. "As soon Zhang's last truck pulls out of here, get down to the yard and start moving our shipment up here. Bring them in the order I showed you, and be careful. Let me know when you back up to the dock." Then he went back to the office.

When the first truck arrived, he met it at the loading dock, and directed the men where to put each of the three crates, then the same with the second truck. The third truck had four crates.

After all ten crates were in the building and secured, Gomez and Zhang opened each one to inspect the contents and prepared them for distribution. The last four crates had to be broken down into smaller containers.

✎•✎

Steve's plane landed in Caracas and taxied to the appointed place, where Fonzie waited in a large box truck. They transferred their gear, and left the airport.

"They were busy this morning, moving a lot of freight," Fonzie said.

"I hope they enjoyed it, that'll be their last shipment," Steve replied.

They arrived at the back door of their office space, late afternoon. "Joe, just bring in the provisions, we won't be here for long."

Then they all went to the window in the front, where Fonzie had his surveillance gear set up. "Now we just watch and wait. We'll move in at midnight."

At ten o'clock, they brought in their gear, laid out their weapons, donned their black-attack uniforms, and made the final preparations to make the move. At midnight, they loaded into the box truck. Fonzie drove through the warehouse complex to the rear of The Bloody Dragon. All was calm and quiet.

Steve picked the lock on the back door, and they entered the building. The warehouse was lit with dim nightlight.

Vic and Zack quickly found the cameras and diverted the view with an electronic loop. Joe and Fonzie unloaded the necessary gear from the truck, while Steve, Clint, and Trevor began opening the crates.

Vic and Zack opened their cases and laid out handcuffs, ropes, gags, and sedatives. Joe and Fonzie started photographing the crates and their contents.

When Steve, Clint, and Trevor finished opening the crates, they went to the office, started disconnecting computers, fax machines, and took them to the truck. They loaded boxes with hard files and paperwork. All of that was loaded into the truck as evidence.

When Vic and Zack finished with the prisoner containment gear, the started setting and wiring explosives on the crates.

Fonzie moved the truck away from the back door so that no one would suspect unusual activity in that warehouse space if they arrived at the back door. By the time morning twilight broke everything was calm and quiet, both in and outside the building. The team watched and listened at the ready, waiting for the first arrivals of the day.

The events of that tragic day in Port Aransas replayed in Steve's mind.

"They're moving about six knots, Colonel."

"Match 'em. Take us in closer. We have to get closer. Drop the rope. Come on pilot, closer, closer. Maintain your position. First man down . . . go! Second man down . . . go!"

"Colonel, I see some activity on the . . . ."

The sound of a key turning a deadbolt broke the silence, and pulled Steve back to reality. Two male voices were laughing and talking as the door swung open. The morning light silhouetted them in the dooeway.

Before either one could make a sound, Vic bashed the butt of his AR into the face of the first man. He went down. Zack grabbed the collar of the second man and knocked him out with one blow from his fist—dragged him inside, and closed the door.

They quickly dragged the two men through the office and the warehouse to the back door, where they tied them up, gagged them, and immobilized them. Vic stayed with them. Zack returned to the front.

It wasn't long until they heard a vehicle pull up in front of the office and shut down. Two car-doors opened and closed. Two voices approached the door. It opened.

Clint took the first man down without a sound. Trevor grabbed the second man, jerked him inside, twisted his arm behind his back, and put a chokehold on him.

Steve closed the door. Then he grabbed the man's face with his left hand, slapped the cigar out of his mouth with his right hand, and said, "Gomez! You fat, little, bald man. I'm the last man on Earth you wanted to see today." Then he knocked him out with one blow from his fist.

Fifteen minutes later, another vehicle pulled up. Two car-doors opened and closed. The office door opened. Steve stood in the center of the room. The first man was a big Chinaman. He took a step inside before he saw Steve. Then he took a Kung Fu pose. Simultaneously, as Steve raised his forty-five, Trevor stepped from behind the door, grabbed the Chinaman, and broke his neck. He dropped to the floor like a wet noodle.

Steve's gun was pointed at the face of the second man. "Come on in, Zhang, we've been waiting for you."

Trevor grabbed him, twisted his arm behind his back, and led him to the back door.

"Get the truck, we're done here," Steve said to Fonzie.

They headed to the airport.

As the truck pulled up to the plane, Steve said, "Keep it running, Fonzie. Fire up the plane, Joe."

The transfer from the truck to plane was quick and smooth. Steve thanked Fonzie, and he drove away. Joe taxied to the runway and shoved the throttle forward. When the wheels left the ground, Zack pulled a little black box out of his pocket and handed it to Steve.

"I'm gonna enjoy this. Take a look, guys." And with that, he flipped the switch. In the distance, a huge fireball rose in the sky. "No more Bloody Dragon in Caracas!"

Joe banked the plane to the north and headed out over the Caribbean.

All the prisoners were sedated, except Gomez, who Steve constantly interrogated and slightly tortured with pleasure. "You thought you got away with it, didn't ya!" He slapped Gomez across the face, causing blood to trickle down from his lower lip. "Do you even know what happened to those two freighters in Texas?"

Gomez said nothing.

"I'm going to make you talk, son of a bitch. Either that or you'll never talk again. Your choice." He slapped him again. "You only have a couple of hours to make up your mind. Do you know where we're going—Texas! They don't like you very much over there. I don't like you very much right now."

Gomez said nothing.

"Do you want to loosen him up a little, Trevor?"

"Thank you, Steve."

Steve went to the bar and poured himself a shot of Jack Daniels.

Trevor pulled a length of rope out of his pocket, wrapped it around Gomez's neck, and twisted it. Then he jerked him to his feet and slammed him against the wall of the plane. He pulled his knife from its sheath and raised it to Gomez's throat, applying just enough pressure to bring blood on the razor sharp edge. "Say something, anything."

"What do you want me to say?" He could only whisper.

"Did you send those freighters to Texas," Steve asked.

Trevor loosened the rope a little, but kept the knife in place.

"I only asked for a little help," Gomez said.

"Who did you ask?"

Gomez rolled his eyes toward Zhang.

Steve took a few steps and kicked Zhang in the head with the heel of his boot, which sent him rolling on the floor. He came to. His eyes rolled around in his head.

Steve went back to Gomez. "Do you even know what happened in Texas?"

"No."

"I'll tell you. One of those ships exploded. I was there. You killed four of my men, and put me in the hospital for months. You're gonna pay for that, son of a bitch!" The he hit him in the gut with all his might. "Let him go."

Trevor loosened the rope, and tossed Gomez to the floor like a sack of potatoes. "You ain't seen nothing yet, asshole!" Trevor took a shot of Jack.

Steve went to the cockpit, sat in the co-pilot seat, and put on the headset. He looked out the window at the gulf. "I really do want to dump that dude in the gulf."

"I knew that when you loaded that chain," Joe said.

"What would you do?"

"Do you want to dump all of them or just the one? If we would have had to kill them to capture them that's one thing, but to take 'em alive and then kill them is another. I've known you for a long time, been through a lot of battles with ya. You're not a murderer, Steve. When I suggested dumping him in the gulf, it was just wishful thinking."

Steve reached up to the instrument panel and flipped a switch. "Operator, will you please dial . . .." Then he took off the headset, shook Joe's hand, and went back to the cabin.

When Joe landed at Johnson Space Center and taxied to the hangar, there were two black sedans, a black van, and two Houston Police cruisers waiting for them. United States Marshals transferred the prisoners to the van, and they all sped away with emergency lights flashing.

He congratulated his team. "Thanks, guys. That was a perfect mission. I have suites for you to stay in tonight. We'll take you home in the morning, but tonight, we celebrate." So, they unloaded Steve's gear from the plane, and went into the conference room.

Steve pulled a magnum of Champaign from the refrigerator. He filled the glasses and passed out cigars. "Men, these dudes that we captured today are just a small part of an organized, global crime ring that spreads terror everywhere they exist. We did our part in cleaning up a tiny bit of that scum.

"I've been assured by the Attorney General that the charges against each of these thugs will be extensive, including terrorism against the United States.

"More to the point, we attained a measure of redemption with this mission. These thugs were directly responsible for the death of four of our comrades in arms. In that, we can express personal satisfaction. A toast, gentlemen, to those who fight the good fight of good against evil, especially those that pay the ultimate sacrifice." And the glasses clinked.

After a night on the town and a good night's sleep, Joe flew the team back to Corpus Christi, and Steve went to the Federal Courthouse in downtown Houston to file his report. Then he drove to Port Aransas.

ॐ•ॐ

Jacob and Michelle were having lunch on the deck. It was an unusually warm winter day.

"Someone just pulled into our driveway," Michelle said.

Jacob got up and went down the steps to see who it was. Steve and Chelsea met him at the corner of the house. "Hey, we wondered what was happening." They went up to the table on the deck.

"Well, I've got good news," Steve started to say. "But, I see you already know." There was a newspaper lying on the table. "Nice headline, 'Texas Terrorists Arrested in Caracas.'"

"Good news travels fast. How'd it go?"

"It was perfect. Everything fell right into place."

"Of course, the article is vague. Give us some details. I haven't talked to you since I left Houston. So, how did it go down?"

"There were six of us, some of the same guys that went with me to rescue Destiny. We went to Caracas two days ago. My CIA contact there did a fabulous job of setting everything up for us. He rented an office space, across the warehouse row from a Chinese organization called The Bloody Dragon. That's where Gomez went when he left Nicaragua. They are the ones that supplied the two ships and explosives that came to Texas."

"Really."

"So, we watched and waited in that office until midnight, then we made our move. It was perfect timing. They had just received a new shipment of all kinds of counterfeit electronics, lady's fashion accessories, weapons, and explosives. It was a jackpot of evidence. We just waited by the front door for them to come in. When they did, we grabbed them, took them to the back, and tied them up."

"You didn't have to shoot any of them?"

"Well, we killed one of them, a Chinese. He thought he was going to put some Kung Fu on us—Trevor broke his neck. We brought five back with us. But, during the night, we set some of our own explosives." He took a picture out of his pocket and laid it on the table.

"Wow, that's awesome!"

"I flipped the switch when we took off."

"So, no more Bloody Dragon?"

"Not in Caracas, but they're a global crime ring. Maybe we haven't heard the last of them. But, now it's the responsibility of the State Department and National Intelligence."

"Way to go, Steve, thank you. What's in the bag?"

"Do you have to ask?" He pulled a bottle of Champaign from the bag and a couple of cigars from his pocket.

"I know what to do now," Michelle said, and she went to get some glasses and an ashtray.

After the traditional toast, and the lighting of the cigars, Steve said, "But, that's not all of the story."

"What could be better than that?" Michelle asked.

"I am now, undeniably, retired. Show 'em, Chelsea."

She laid her left hand on the table, with a large, shimmering diamond on her ring finger.

Michelle screamed, jumped up, and threw her arms around Chelsea's neck, and the two girls began to bawl like a couple of giddy children. Jacob did the same to Steve, but with jubilation instead of bawling.

"Okay, you guys, this calls for another toast," Jacob said. So, they all raised their glasses. "Chelsea, Paradise is going to be jealous of you." They all laughed. "But, she'll get over that. Here's to the union of two of the finest people I've ever known. To Steve and Chelsea!" And the glasses clinked. And the celebration began.

"Have you told Jesse yet about Gomez?" Chelsea asked.

"No. He doesn't have a phone."

"We can send an email to Alley," Michelle said. "I'm sure she'd like to see a picture of this ring too." And the girls took off to the office.

"So, Steve, no more gallivanting around the world, chasing hardened criminals, huh?"

"Hey, there's nothing glamorous about it. I've been shot at, stabbed, run over, and knocked out more than my share of times. I served my country to the best of my ability. That explosion got my attention. The world is changing, and I'm not getting any younger."

"I hear ya, any regrets?"

"I just wish there was a way to stop people before they do their dirty deeds, instead of just capturing them after the fact."

"Well, it sounds like that's what you just did."

Steve raised his eyebrows and took another drink.

"So, was this a spur of the moment kind of thing or how far have you thought it out. Where do you go from here?"

"Oh, the thought entered my mind in the hospital Then again in Saint Croix. Looking back, I think God gave me the opportunity for one last fling, and to go out with a bang. It just worked out that way. I got the message."

"I'm sure Chelsea is thrilled."

"She's the one that made me see the light. On the island, we danced around the idea, and she let me know we could never take the next step as long as I was flirting with disaster. I let it go at that. The other day, flying back from Caracas, the light bulb went off in my head."

"It sounds like a rational conclusion. What about Joe?"

"He can stay at JSC, working with the fleet of astronaut's T-8s.

I'll sell my place in Houston, and move down here with Chelsea. Money's not a problem, so we'll start looking for a house."

"Oh, really." Jacob took a drink and leaned back in his chair.

The girls came back outside. "Alley is so excited about all the news. She's happy for you, Steve. She'll tell Jesse the good news," Michelle said.

"Michelle, Steve just told me that he's moving down here and they want to get a house."

"Are you thinking what I'm thinking?" she said.

"Probably." He set her up.

"Steve, why don't you consider building?"

"I haven't spent a lot of time here, but from what I've seen there isn't a lot of empty space for new houses."

"That's because you've overlooked the prime real-estate."

"What do you mean?"

"Have you ever wondered why we don't have any neighbors? We own ten acres of waterfront property. It goes way down there by Dan's place." She pointed south. "It just makes sense. Chelsea works here. We love you both. You could even be out of rock throwing distance. It just makes sense."

Chelsea perked up and looked at Steve with puppy dog eyes.

"Okay, okay," Jacob said. "The offer is on the table. They already have a lot to think about in the coming days and weeks. Y'all talk about it. Any time you want, we can drive down there and walk the land. You know what, we need to get the rest of the gang over here and have a party." So, he made a few phone calls. Then Steve and he fired up the barbecue pit.

Michelle and Chelsea took some steaks and fish out of the freezer and went to the store before prepping for a small feast.

Steve had to tell his story repeatedly. The last one was to Paradise, when she came home from school. He and Chelsea walked her down to Paradise Cove to tell her the big news, while Michelle watched from the deck to see her reaction.

ও•ও

Michelle was full of emotion as she watched for Paradise's reaction, not that she was worried about her, but she just didn't know what to expect. As she sat on the edge of her chair, leaning on the rail of the deck, her mind shut out all the partying that went on around her, and she focused her radar on Paradise Cove.

Chelsea and Paradise sat on a bench and Steve knelt in front of them. Michelle could only see Steve's face—he spoke to Paradise. Shortly after, Paradise showed a brief moment of celebration.

He must have told her about the capture, Michelle thought. *Here comes the big news.*

By then, the dolphins appeared curious and gathered in front of the bench. Every once in a while, one of the dolphins turned its head askant like a puppy dog when it hears something unfamiliar.

Then Chelsea showed Paradise her ring, and the two embraced.

I can't tell if she's happy or sad, Michelle thought.

Then Steve spoke to paradise again, and she leaped like a frog onto Steve, locking her arms around his neck. Steve stood and the two whirled around in circles a few times.

He must have told her that he is moving here, she thought.

Then the three of them headed back toward the party arm in arm. About half way up the slope, Paradise took off running.

Michelle could see her face clearly. *Those are tears of joy*, she thought. By the time she made it down the steps to ground level, Paradise embraced her, full of emotion.

"It's so awesome," Paradise said. "It's what I always wanted. We're all going to be together."

Michelle rubbed and patted her back. "I know, baby."

"Isn't that ring beautiful?"

And the party continued into the night.

8 THE PATHS OF LIFE

The days of spring waxed, and Paradise worked hard to graduate with honors. Michelle made sure Paradise had everything she needed to succeed—love, discipline, and encouragement.

A handful of boys jockeyed to court her, and she did allow a couple of them a chance to get closer than before, but the price of a relationship was high. Her available time to play was at a premium.

Occasionally, she woke in the morning tired and dissatisfied with life. "Mom, these extra classes are killing me."

"You should already know that nothing good in life comes easy. Rewards require hard work. It doesn't do it by itself. You have to put in the time and effort to see the results you want."

"I'm tired."

Michelle put an arm around her, pulled her to tight, and kissed her on the head. "You should be tired. If you weren't, you wouldn't be doing enough. You have to go through the fire to get to the other side."

"Mom."

"I know it sounds like a cliché, but it's true. The only way you're going to learn that is by experience. It's not too long or too hard for you to endure. Set your mind to it and get it done. One day, you'll wake up and it'll be in the past. On that day, tell me how you feel. Are you ready for breakfast?"

"Yes."

Jacob came in from outside and joined them for breakfast. "When Chelsea gets here, will y'all go down there and check all the girls?"

"What do you mean?"

"Two of them look like they're getting a little fatter, if you know what I mean."

"Which ones?"

"Providence and Dolly."

"Dolly? Isn't she a little old for that?"

"Well, maybe not too old."

"I've always wondered if we might get a little Sam one day."

"Might be."

"Where are you going?"

Paradise opened the door. "To talk to the girls."

"Why didn't I think of that?" Jacob said with a chuckle.

Paradise returned with a smile, got a cup of coffee, and sat at the counter.

"Well?" Michelle asked.

"Only Dolly. Providence is a little jealous. Sam is a little embarrassed—that was his first time." She blushed.

Michelle and Jacob rolled their eyes at each other and smiled.

"How long ago?" Michelle asked.

"About a month."

"Why are you blushing?"

"Mom!" And she left the kitchen.

It was a Saturday afternoon. Jacob, Michelle, and Greg were taking a lunch break on the deck when Chelsea rounded the corner and joined them.

After the girls chatted for a minute, Jacob interrupted. "Where's Steve?"

"He's at the house. He wants you and Greg to go over there, something about an initiation. He said it's a guy thing. Go around back, he's waiting for ya."

Jacob and Greg looked at each other with raised eyebrows, got up, went to Jacob's truck, and drove away. When they got there, Steve had a big smile.

"Welcome to my new deck, gentlemen. Come on up. We have to break this thing in the right way. They just put in the stairs this morning."

It was a big house, raised on stilts.

"Wow, they're moving right along," Jacob said.

"They're a good crew. Come on in, let's look at this framing."

"Hey, you've got some duct in here," Greg said. "I used to do that. Duct-board was my favorite. It looks like they know what they're doing."

"They said they would finish the rough-in on Monday, and the plumbers are coming in then. The carpenters are through inside. They just have to finish the outside trim and railing on the deck. That's a temporary front door, just to control the wind. Here's the real one over here. Then the electricians, fireplace, and insulation."

"I just love this floor plan," Jacob said. "Does Chelsea help you plan?"

"You bet! She has some good ideas. Let's go back out here." He headed for the deck. There was a makeshift table, some lawn chairs, and an ice chest. He pointed. "Y'all help yourselves. Everything's in there."

"Speaking of plans, have you picked a date?"

"Well, that's part of what I wanted to talk to you about. We're narrowing it down, and both of us think it should be sooner than later. I'll just get to the point . . . can we do it at your place, down at the dock?"

"Thank you, Steve. Absolutely! Michelle's been pushing me to ask you that question. That would mean the world to her. I'm sure that by now, you know how much weddings mean to these girls, and now that the question has been answered, all we have to do is just sit back and let them take over . . . they've already got it planned out."

"Wow, that's a load off my mind. The next question is do you know a preacher?"

"Boy, do I, the best one in the world. Pastor Arnold is a Marine, served in World War II and Korea. He survived the battle of Inch'ŏn. He's not here, he's up in northwest Arkansas, but like you, he has his own plane. We watch him on TV, but we went up there to meet him a few years back."

"And you think he would come down here to do our wedding?"

"Man, when he hears your name and who you are, I bet we couldn't stop him from coming. You will definitely be impressed with this man of God."

"Why didn't you tell me about him before?"

"I didn't want to push it on ya, but now the cat is out of the bag. You want the best. You deserve the best. I'll call him. Then you call him."

"Sounds like a plan."

"Speaking of planes, what are you going to do with yours?"

"What do you mean? It's in a hangar in Corpus."

"No, I mean looking forward."

"Chelsea had the same reaction. I guess I have to explain myself better. When I said 'retired,' I meant from bounty hunting and

Special Ops, but I still have other work. For example, I'm still a military strategist. I retained my rank and clearance. I still have to travel around the world from time to time, but hopefully, I won't get shot at as much."

"Ah, that makes sense."

"So, I'm keeping the plane. That's my plane. I can even take Chelsea to check on some of your places if she needs to go there. She'll have her own body guard."

They chuckled.

"Now there's something we can talk about later," Jacob said."

"Chelsea?"

"No, Paradise."

No more was said for a few minutes, as the three sipped their bourbon and puffed their cigars, gazing out across the bay from Steve's new deck. The salty fragrance of the morning gulf wafted around the corners of the house, as the relentless Texas wind resumed its daily attack on Port Aransas.

"It's strange, isn't it," Greg said.

"What's that?" Jacob asked.

"The different paths we all took that led to the same place."

"And here we sit together," Steve said.

"Yeah," Jacob said. "Our paths converged here, but others will diverge from here."

They fell silent again and sipped and puffed and gazed.

ဆာ•ၡ

Paradise, Michelle, and Chelsea sat on the dock with their feet hung over the edge, surrounded by dolphins. Chelsea took a sip of wine, and said, "Paradise, have you given much thought to life after high school? It's not far away, you know."

"Not really, I've been too busy. This is the first time in a long time that I've been able to do this."

"Aside from the rest of your life, what about the days and weeks after graduation? Isn't there something special that you want to do?"

"Yeah, there is, but I think it would cost too much."

"You can let us worry about that," Michelle said. "What is it?"

"Well, I want to do like we did a couple of summers ago, when we went to the different Ocean Masters, but there are some places in the world where dolphins really need help. Now that we know about all the sanctuaries around the world, it would be easy to plot a course. And with God's help, and Jarrell's help, we could change the life of a lot of dolphins and whales. That's what I want to do."

"I figured you'd say something like that," Chelsea said. "Michelle, that would be easy for us to plan, wouldn't you say?"

"I think so."

"Let's see, travel would be the biggest expense. Let's see, who do we know that has a plane and the time to fly us around the world?"

"Uncle Steve has a plane," she said as she perked up.

"You know, I think you've got something there young lady. And I just happen to know that he has a lot of extra time on his hands. Now that I think of it, a trip like that would kill two birds with one stone." She smiled and winked at Michelle.

Michelle returned the smile and wink. "Honeymoon! We've got a lot of planning to do." The two ladies headed for the house.

Paradise remained on the dock with the dolphins playing at her feet. After a few minutes, she heard that soft, gentle voice say, "you better go with them and tell them where we're going."

She looked around, but no one was there. "Thank you, Father." She ran up to the house.

With just a week to graduation day, Chelsea said, "Michelle, there's so much to think about, it's chaotic! I don't know how you keep it together."

"You don't see behind the scenes. Almost every morning, I throw my hands up in the air and scream. Then I get my first cup of coffee. It's all downhill after that."

"But seriously, Jacob has had to deal with finals-week and graduations for a long time, but now you add Paradise into the mix. Then a wedding, and two weeks around the world, and you still don't have any gray hair."

"Well."

"If we figured it right, when we get back our house will be ready to move in to. I think I'm gonna need a vacation from the vacation."

They both chuckled.

"That's the way it always works. You think you're getting away from the rat-race, but when you break your daily routine at home all you're doing is stepping into the fire."

"And that requires a little recovery, doesn't it?"

"You got it."

ಒ•ಲ

They stood outside of the high school building just before Paradise's graduation ceremony.

"Well, my little girl, you're not so little anymore," Jacob said. "It seems like it's been a long time, but you got it done in eleven years instead of twelve. How does it feel?"

"I don't know, Dad. Right now, this all seems like part of the journey. It still doesn't feel like it's over yet. I think it's going to have to sink in."

He gave her a big hug and kissed her on the head.

"Thank you, Dad."

Then it was Michelle's turn. "You know how much of a honor it is to be Class Valedictorian. Be humble and respectful to everyone around you. Your classmates, teachers, and you have been a team throughout this journey. They are all part of your life. Don't forget that. We're so proud of you."

And they hugged.

"Mom, don't make me cry." She laughed to hold back the tears.

"Okay, we'll see you when it's over."

When it all was over, before she could exit the auditorium, Mr. Jarvis stopped her and gave her a hug. "Paradise, in all of my years, I haven't had another student like you. I'm going to miss your smile and enthusiasm in my class. You have a bright future in front of you. You know where to find me. Please, don't let this be the end of our friendship."

"Don't worry, Sir. I could never forget you. You can't get rid of me this easy. Who knows, maybe we'll have another baby dolphin in your spring pool."

They laughed and hugged.

Steve and Chelsea waited outside with Jacob and Michelle, when Paradise and her friends walked out of the school doors for the last time.

"Well, Paradise," Steve said. "You've only just begun, now the fun starts, but you'll always be my little girl."

She threw herself at him, buried her face in his chest, and started to cry.

After the embrace, he said, "Can we take you and your friends to dinner before you go party?"

The girls nodded.

❧•❧

Steve and Chelsea got married in a private ceremony on the Anderson's dock, over the water, surrounded by friends and dolphins. Then they took Jacob's boat across the bay to the Corpus

Christi T-Head Pier, where they were picked up by a handsome-cab and carted to a downtown hotel.

They spent the night in the honeymoon suite and returned home the next day.

9 SEA CHANGE

Michelle came home from a morning of shopping. Paradise and Chelsea were in the office, researching facilities and cities they planned to visit on their upcoming trip.

She plopped an armful of stuff down on the kitchen counter, and said, "Paradise, will you help with the groceries? I've got something else for you."

Paradise and Chelsea came into the kitchen. "What is it?" Paradise asked.

Michelle pointed at a stack of envelopes on the counter. "You're a popular girl these days."

"Oh man! They just won't stop, will they?"

"At least you have choices," Chelsea said. "Most kids have to plead and beg to get into any university, and never even get close to the one of their choice."

"Well, this would be great if I wanted to go to a university full of ignorant, liberal professors that want to shove the big bang theory, the theory of evolution, and the theory of global warming down my throat—ain't gonna happen!"

"I hear ya, sister."

"There aren't very many Christian schools that have credible marine biology programs with emphasis on Cetaceans. Y'all know that. I've already received answers from the three queries I sent. I just have to decide which one."

"That's a good position to be in."

Paradise threw the bundle of letters in the trash, smiled, and went out to the car for some more groceries.

Chelsea got a cup of coffee. "I'm working on an introductory package that we can pass out to anyone we find on the trip that shows any interest in DolphinWorks. I could use your input."

"Sure, I'll be there in a few minutes," Michelle said.

ം•ഏ

All the luggage, gear, and hardware were loaded on the plane and their vehicles were secured in the hangar. Paradise, Michelle, and Chelsea prepared for take off in the cabin, while Jacob and Steve manned the cockpit.

"It's amazing how much stuff a woman takes on a trip," Steve said.

Jacob chuckled. "You figured that one out already, huh?"

"Yeah. So you've sat in that seat before, do you remember what Joe told you?"

"Yeah."

"We'll go over it again anyway." Steve fired up the engines, and went over instructions with Jacob. Then he went back to the cabin to make sure the ladies were ready and secure for take off.

He contacted the tower, taxied to the runway, and pushed his intercom button. "Is everyone ready? Next stop, Bermuda." Then he shoved the throttle forward, and in a few short minutes the Corpus Christi skyline grew smaller and smaller until it disappeared from view.

When they landed in Bermuda, they picked up the rental van and drove to the hotel. That night, they toured the town and ate at a restaurant on the beach.

The next day, they took care of business with a visit to the famous, local dolphinarium, Dolphin Chest.

"Places like this really piss me off," Jacob said. "They tag a few dolphins, pay a flunky to tabulate the tag-data, and use that to justify the exploitation of their captive animals."

"That'll change today," Michelle said.

At the entrance gate, Paradise heard a whisper. "We're with you, Paradise. Use your gift, in Christ's Name!"

Chelsea asked an employee for the location of the facility office. "I want to leave this business package for the director."

"Follow me, "she said.

Chelsea and Michelle went with the girl, while the other three waited on a bench.

The girl opened the door. "Right in here, Ma'am. Would you like for me to wait for you?"

"No, that will be fine. Thank you." They went in.

The receptionist asked, "How may I help you?"

"We represent a company in the States that researches Cetaceans, and we'd like to leave this package for the Director."

"He is out of the office at this time. Would you care to arrange a meeting?"

"That won't be necessary at this time."

"What is your business?"

"We research wild and captive Cetaceans."

"Who is your principal investigator?"

"Dr. Jacob Anderson."

"Oh, I've heard of him. Is he here today? Will you be attending our dolphin show at eleven?"

"Yes, we will."

"Fine then. I'll leave this on the director's desk, and I hope you enjoy the show."

"Oh, we will."

They slowly made their way to the arena and found seats front and center. There was a small crowd of about fifty people in attendance. Five bottlenose dolphins casually milled about the pool.

The stadium music picked up, and two dolphin trainers ran to the platform at the front and center of the pool. All five dolphins breached simultaneously and sped around the perimeter of the pool.

"Ladies and gentlemen, welcome to our show! We are privileged to have a famous dolphin scientist in the audience today, Dr. Jacob Anderson!"

The dolphins lined up in the center of the pool, stood on their tail flukes, and waved their pectoral fins.

"Dr. Anderson, will you give us a wave?"

Jacob rolled his eyes at Michelle, stood, and waved. When he sat down, he mumbled, "They shouldn't have done that. Let 'em have it, Paradise."

Seconds after she started her *dolphin whisper*, all five dolphins stopped what they were doing and left the arena, to the trainers' dismay.

"I guess they're ready for a break." The girl tried to keep the attention focused.

The audience laughed.

She called the dolphins by name, one by one, but they did not return.

The audience became restless, disappointed, and began filing out of the arena.

"Well, our job is done here. Let's get out of here," Jacob said.

They went straight to the airport. Steve's plane had been serviced and refueled overnight. "Y'all start loading it up. I'll do my preflight check."

It didn't take long before they were wheels-up.

"Next stop, Antibes, France," Jacob said.

"I hate France," Steve said.

"Why?"

"They're weasels! Well, I don't mean to insult the weasel family—even they have a backbone. You'd know what I mean if you ever had to fight with or against them. Maybe that means just the few in my experience. I'd hate to throw the whole country into that lot. It's my experience that they'd rather surrender than fight, no courage."

Jacob raised his eyebrows and nodded. "I'll remember that if we get in a fight." He smiled.

"OH, they're quick to start a fight, but all you have to do is slap 'em across the face and they'll start whimpering."

They landed at Antibes at dusk, rented a van, and went to the hotel.

"What do you want to do tonight, Paradise," Michelle asked. "Do you want to go out and see the town?"

"I don't think so, Mom. My gut tells me this isn't a vacation for fun. I just want to go to bed, get up in the morning, and take care of business."

"You're a wise girl," Steve said. "You have the mentality of a warrior. I always knew you were special." He hugged her and kissed her on the head.

"We'll order-in tonight, if that's alright with everyone," Jacob said.

They all agreed.

The next morning, they had breakfast in the lobby.

"One little change of plans," Chelsea said. "Let's find out where the nearest post office is. I'd rather just mail this package to them than go to their office."

"Good idea," Michelle said. "We'll do that from now on. These places we're going to are our enemy. It's hard enough just to walk through the facilities. Let's not overload our donkey."

"I'll go a step further," Jacob said. "I'll introduce myself at the gate and request a behind the scenes tour. If that works, we won't even have to watch a show."

It was the perfect situation—the girl that led them on the tour could speak only broken English. She had no knowledge of the individual animals just what it took to produce a dolphin show. And, she had no clue as to what the Andersons were up to. She played right into their hands.

It was easy for Paradise to lag behind and talk to the dolphins, whales, and pinnipeds. Her message remained true from the beginning, Stop performing for your captors, and get released.

At the end of the tour, they left the facility. There were no more shows to see.

On the way to the airport, Steve asked Paradise, "Your gift of communicating with animals is astonishing. How do you think it works?"

"I thought about that too, so I asked Sam one day. He said the only people that have been able to communicate with animals has been God and the angels."

"Ah—Elohim."

"Yeah, so when they understand the language coming out of a flesh-human's mouth they stop, listen, and take heed."

Chelsea's head went askant. "Wait a minute, say that again."

Paradise recapitulated.

Everyone else in the van tweaked their head askant when they heard Paradise say that.

"Wait a minute," Steve said. "That makes it clear. That means that your gift is at least a form of the cloven tongue. Have you ever tried it on humans?"

A soft, gentle voice filled the van. "It is not permitted at this time. That time has not yet come!"

Steve pulled to the edge of the road, slammed on the brakes, and looked in the review mirror. Then he turned to look at the others, who had the same look on their faces as he did—except Paradise, who had a smile. "Was that what I think it was?" He asked.

She shrugged her shoulders and raised her eyebrows.

Steve pulled away from the curb and continued. Not another word was spoken.

After they visited all the planned sites in Europe, there were two major stops left on the agenda. They continued west on their trip around the world, which brought them to the small fishing and whaling town of Taiji, Japan.

"Y'all know why we had to come here?" Paradise asked.

"They kill dolphins," Steve said.

"No, Uncle Steve, They slaughter dolphins. These people have a long historical record of murdering whales and dolphins even before time was recorded—God knows, and He doesn't forget.

"He has sent many to deal with the problem, but none have succeeded. Now it's time to end their wicked behavior. Many peoples have killed whales for food and oil throughout time, but these people have distorted even that. They have allowed their false religion to tell them that dolphins are their enemies. They actually believe that in order for them to survive, all the dolphins must die."

"That's perverted!" Jacob said. "What are we gonna do?"

"This won't take too long. You and I are going to the harbor, and the rest of you wait here. We're not here to negotiate. I have to speak to the sea, and then we must leave quickly. I just know that's going to happen. I don't know what else is going to happen."

"Paradise?" Michelle said with a shaky voice.

"Don't worry, Mom. There are ten thousand angels watching over us. We have all the protection we need." They hugged.

"Let's go and get this over with," Jacob said.

Jacob and Paradise rented a car, got a map with directions to the harbor, and left the airport. The road to town was small and wound downward through a thickly wooded hillside until the trees cleared and the majestic Pacific Ocean consumed their view.

In front of them was the small town of Taiji, set on the hillside, on the banks of a cove, as if it were built on the side of a funnel, which the ocean naturally drained into.

She pointed. "That's where we're going, Dad."

"Man, they must be having some kind of celebration. I didn't think there were this many people in this town." He drove through the obstacle filled streets.

They came to the parking lot of the docks that Paradise had pointed out. As the car stopped, she said, "Dad! That's Jarrell."

He opened Paradise's door. "Jacob. You wait here. Come with me, Paradise."

They followed a path up a hill to an overlook, disappearing from Jacob's sight.

"It looks like they're having a party," She said.

"Once a year, neighboring towns gather here to kick off the annual dolphin hunt, and to bless the kill before the boats depart. It's a two-day celebration. That is why you are here now. Father's timing is perfect. Look out over this ocean. These people have been senselessly slaughtering the dolphins in this ocean for millennia, and Father has had enough."

"But, why me? What can I do?"

"He doesn't need your help, but this is part of His plan. He wants you to know what will happen here. This is one of your rings of life."

"What do I do?"

"Speak to the ocean. Tell the life within it to start now, to move out to sea. A change is about to take place. Speak now."

"I don't know what to say."

"Let the Spirit speak through you."

When she had finished, he gently grabbed her arm and led her back down the hill, saying, "It has begun. Let us away!"

By the time they got to the car, it started raining. He opened her door and she got in. "Go back to your plane. Leave this land. Do not look back." And he disappeared.

As they drove back up the hill, lightening began to strike Taiji and it burned. Jacob drove frantically, the earth rumbling behind them.

He drove right past the terminal to the plane. They jumped out and boarded it.

"Go, Steve! Go! Get the hell out of here!"

"Man! What did Y'all do?"

"We'll tell ya later, just go!"

"You got it, cowboy. On to Hawaii."

By the time they arrived at their hotel for the night, the world's Press Corp swarmed around Taiji, Japan. The hotel lobby and registration desk buzzed with the news.

Jacob asked the desk clerk, "What's going on around here?"

"Haven't you heard? A whole town in Japan has been abolished! There's nothing left, just a bare footprint of the town that used to be there."

"Can we get our keys, we have reservations."

"Yes, sir. I'm sorry for all the confusion, but there was an undersea earthquake and we've been waiting to see if we need to evacuate!"

"There's no need to worry," Paradise said. "It's not coming over here." But, the man ignored the truth.

"If you'll wait just a minute, a bellhop will assist you."

"That's fine. Where's the bar?"

The man pointed.

"Girls, wait here. Come on, Steve." They went to the bar and ordered some beverages to be delivered upstairs, then they went up. They gathered in Jacob and Michelle's suite.

Jacob turned on the television just in time to catch the

beginning of the news cycle. The reporter was live on the scene.

"I'm standing at the top of the hill, looking down at the landscape of what used to be the town of Taiji, Japan. It's an eerie site to behold because from this vantage point there is no evidence that a town was ever here."

The camera panned down the hillside toward the ocean.

"Reports flooded the cyber-world about a freakish storm that blew in from the ocean, bringing torrential rains and lightning that set the town of Taiji on fire.

"This happened at a time during the annual celebration to kick off the traditional fishing season."

"Did you hear that?" Chelsea said. "He called it a fishing season!"

Emergency vehicles sped past the reporter. He continued, "When the storm hit, the crowds of people fled for cover. The reports of an earthquake at sea, sparking an enormous tsunami, inundated the media's airwaves.

"So far, there is only one survivor. This is file footage of his interview: 'Sir, did you witness the destruction of this town?'"

"I saw the whole thing."

"Dad! That's Jarrell!"

"When the storm hit, everyone else went in the buildings for cover, but I went up on that hilltop." He pointed. "There was nothing I could do to save anyone. I watched the town burn to the ground, as the rains flooded the streets and hillside, washing debris and bodies into the cove.

"Then the earth began to rumble and shake. The ocean became angry. A huge tidal-wave funneled right up into this little canyon, submerged the whole town, and dragged it back into the sea. Everything was gone. Nothing was left. Then the sea calmed. The storm calmed, and the sun shown. Here we stand. If I were you, I wouldn't go down there because I don't think its over yet."

"Dad! Did you hear what he said? It's not over yet."

"That appears to be the lone survivor of the devastation that took place here, but oddly enough, we can't find him any more. It's as if he vanished into thin air. Reporting live from what used to be Taiji, Japan."

Jacob muted the television. Room service arrived and left. "I think we all need to take a deep breath, talk to God, and then I'm gonna have a drink."

So they did.

Then Michelle asked, "Paradise, what did you do when y'all went down into that town?"

"Mom! I had nothing to do with the destruction of that town."

"Can you tell us what was said when you went up on that hilltop with Jarrell?" Jacob asked.

"He told me that God brought me there to see the place before He changed it. He didn't tell me how it would change, just that it would. Then he told me to speak to the sea."

"What did you say to the sea?"

"He told me to tell the life within to flee the shore and go out to sea. That's what I did. Then we left, and the storm started. I don't feel bad about what happened to those people—they brought it on themselves. I didn't destroy them—God did. I don't know why y'all are so surprised. It's not like He hasn't done this sort of thing before, remember Sodom and Gomorrah . . . and Noah . . . and the Katabole?"

They all sat quietly, contemplating. Then Steve spoke up. "This is awesome. It could be overwhelming, to think that we are the only people on Earth that truly knows what took place today. We've learned a great deal. Some of it is obvious in the moment, but I'm sure that in the days, weeks, and months to come, more will be realized about what happened on this day."

"It's easy to see how the media is going to spin this," Chelsea said. "They won't face the facts about the immoral, wicked behavior those people have perpetrated for time on end. Even in their liberal essence of environmental activism and animal cruelty, rather than reporting the crimes against nature by the people of Taiji, the media is going to call for compassion, and a global effort to assist in the restoration of Taiji. That's how sick and twisted the media is these days."

"Let them have it," Michelle said. "They can cry, pout, and moan all they want to. We know God is in control. They can't outsmart God, and they can't beat God. They try to every day."

Chelsea opened up. "Well, I'm sure we've all had fantasies about what should happen to those people, at some point, but now we see God's resolve. I know that whatever God does is the best possible thing that can be done. All we have to do now is thank Him for His wisdom, justice, and resolve, and know that we don't have to think about that issue any longer."

"Amen to that!" Michelle said.

"I don't know about y'all," Steve said, as he walked over to the balcony doors and pulled open the shades. "The more I think about it, the more I'm invigorated by the prospects. I think it's safe to say that we have the right to celebrate a little bit—not at the loss of life today, but at the manner in which it was conducted."

"I agree with that," Jacob said, and they clinked their glasses.

"So, we're down to our last two stops," Michelle said. "Tomorrow, we visit the large dolphinarium here, then it's on to San Diego."

"How do you feel about traveling around the world, Paradise?" Steve asked.

"I'm exhausted."

They all laughed.

"Wait a minute," Jacob said, and he turned up the volume on the television.

The news anchorman said, "We're sending you back to our correspondent in Taiji for some breaking news."

"Things have become frantic here for the first-responders. As they started searching the outer edges of the scarred earth for any evidence of survivors, the earth began to rumble and shake again. So, they've all retreated here to the top of the hill for their own safety. And now, we're all just watching and waiting to see what will happen next. But wait, oh no! This is a stronger aftershock. We have to move back."

The camera stayed live as the crew moved back.

"You are seeing this live, folks," the reporter continued. "Oh no! What did these people do to deserve total destruction? The entire hillside has collapsed into the harbor, filling the basin, and driving the water out into the Pacific Ocean. All of a sudden, just feet in front of me, what used to be a hillside with a town on it is now a sheer cliff of hundreds of feet, un-navigable, and isolated.

"The ocean seems to be boiling as the earth still shakes. It appears as though heaps of sharp, pointed rocks are rising and jutting out of the water randomly scattered closely together for hundreds of feet out in the ocean. From this viewpoint, it looks like no boat, no matter how small, could navigate through the field of jagged rocks. The town of Taiji, Japan is no more. It is totally obliterated."

Jacob muted the television again. "Well, it looks like God put His explanation point on it. The actions of those people brought down the wrath of God on them."

"Jarrell warned them," Paradise said. "The last thing he said in his interview was, 'it isn't over yet.'"

"Now it's over and done!" Steve said. "Those people can just go home. There's nothing left for them to do, but marvel."

"So Steve, do you have any problem with us going to the Navy base in a couple of days? We don't know what will happen there," Michelle asked.

He sat back and thought for a minute. "I did receive training with dolphins there a long time ago. That's where I learned how amazing they are. That's also where I developed my ill-feelings toward their captivity. So no, I have no problem with it. I'd be a fool to argue with God's judgement. I'll get you on the base—whatever happens, happens."

After a couple of days in Hawaii, they continued their journey eastward around the world, which took them back them back to the mainland of the United States and California.

At breakfast, Steve had something to say. "Regardless of what I said last night, I've been discussing the matter with myself." He hesitated. "The truth is, I've been arguing with myself. I have to keep convincing me that I am not attacking the United States Navy, of which I am a Life-long member. The answer always goes back to one comforting thought—God's will is the only thing that matters, that's it. It's so easy. If ya just give a problem to Him, He'll take all the pressure off you. From then on, it's His problem, and He'll take care of it however He sees fit.

"If He didn't want me here, I wouldn't be here. I say this to God—Father, bless America and bless the captive animals."

A ranking officer that Steve knew met them at the front gate of the Navy base. He escorted them through the base to the aquatic area known as, SPAWAR. Interpreting to the civilians as they made their way, he said, "You are about to see the main location were the Navy conducts its own personal, individual training of aquatic animals. We do, however, have other animals spread across the country for evaluation and research purposes."

They traveled through the base, passed several checkpoints, and finally came to the large harbor. There were shacks, buildings, and offices on all sides. In front of those buildings, were piers and docks with warehouses and labs attached. Also connected to those piers and docks, were various holding pens. In those various holding pens, were various marine mammals.

"You are probably wondering about the welfare of the animals. These animals are just like a sailor in the Navy—they are fed, trained, worked, and rested. They lack for nothing."

"But, they are in jail," Paradise said.

"Some sailors may feel the same way," he chuckled.

As soon as I see a dolphin, I'm going to start talking to it, she thought. *Father, what are we going to do here? I mean, what are You going to do here?*

The tour ended, and they left the base.

"Well, that was uneventful," Jacob said.

"It may seem that way," Paradise said. "We'll have to wait and see. That place is different than any other we've visited because of the tight security. We just have to wait and see."

"Did you talk to the animals?"

"I told them to watch for the next opportunity to escape, and when it comes, head south to the sanctuary of the Galapagos Islands."

"You know those animals are all tagged and tracked," Steve said.

"As if that matters to God."

"You know what," Jacob said. "I've been dying to say this . . . let's go home!" And everyone cheered.

ও • ঙ

Sitting at the kitchen bar, Jacob poured a cup of coffee, rubbed his face, and combed the hair out of his eyes with his fingers. "What a wild ride."

Michelle took her head out of the refrigerator. "We have to go to the store this morning."

"Put it on the list. It's nice to be home, huh? I think I slept too much. I feel hung over, but I'm not. Guess I'm just getting old."

"I think it's just called jet-lag."

"Yeah, you're probably right."

"Good morning, Dad." She gave him a kiss on the cheek.

"Good morning, Mom." She gave her mom a hug and a kiss on the cheek. "It's great to be home, isn't it?" She was perked up, vibrant, and already dressed for the day.

Jacob mumbled, "No, I must be getting old."

"What, Dad?"

"Oh nothing. I guess you already have plans for the day?"

"Oh yeah. Can I turn on the TV? I want to catch the news."

It was the top of the hour, and the news cycle was just starting. "Breaking news from California this morning," the newsman said. "This is a developing story, but we can tell you this—the Navy base on the southern coast of California is investigating what happened over night. This is the base where marine mammals are trained to carry out dangerous operations for the Navy. A spokesperson for the base tells reporters that during the night, all the gates to the animal holding pens were suspiciously opened, which allowed all of the marine mammals to escape.

"There is also a report of the sudden development of a red tide that is invading the base's harbor. We'll keep you updated as future reports come in."

Just then, the phone rang, Paradise answered.

"Did you hear that?" Chelsea said. "He did it!"

"I knew something was going to happen, but I didn't know what, when, or how."

"Let me talk to your mom."

"Hey," Michelle said.

"That's some news this morning."

"Yeah, we're just getting up and about."

"Steve has been on the phone for over an hour answering questions from some big wigs. Everything's okay, though, nothing to worry about."

"Wow, well that's good. You know, if those dolphins and whales hadn't left before the red tide moved in, their lives would be in jeopardy."

"I know that. It's amazing. I heard them say earlier that there is no record of a red tide invading that base. They've had them outside the base, but never inside."

"Oh look, he's trying to explain what a red tide is. Wait a minute. What did he just say?" She turned up the volume.

"And so, all the buildings and facilities that are in contact with the water have been evacuated of all military personnel," the reporter said. "There have been red tides around the world throughout history, but never have we seen anything like this—it seems that the dinoflagellates and algae are producing an acidic compound that is rapidly decaying the metal and other materials used for floatation by the Navy in this harbor. Docks and buildings are beginning to sink below the surface, even as I speak."

They clapped and cheered.

"And there you have it," Michelle said. "Thank you, Father! The end of the Navy's Cetacean training program, at least for the time being."

"Michelle, let's not talk about this on the phone anymore. I'll see ya later."

10 AS TIME GOES BY

The Bly's house was finished and furnished. Steve and Chelsea moved in and began a new era together. He continued an abbreviated version of his career. She continued her career with DolphinWorks. Life was good.

They traveled around the world several more times opening new DolphinWorks facilities, holding conferences, and giving speeches about the detriment of Cetacean captivity, and the power of God.

One morning, Steve and Chelsea visited the Andersons. They caught them on the back deck with a bottle of wine and a laptop computer.

"Hey! Look at what the relentless wind blew in," Jacob said.

They all hugged, kissed, and settled around the table.

"You two have been busy—not too busy, I hope," Michelle said.

"Not at all," Chelsea said. "We're having fun. You go ahead, Steve."

"Well . . . uh . . ." He stuttered, uncharacteristically.

"Spit it out, man!" Jacob said.

"I want to invite y'all to Washington with us next week."

"You mean D.C.? Why? What's going on?"

"Well . . . uh, the President wants to give me the Medal of Honor."

"What?" Jacob jumped to his feet. "Are you kidding me? You bet!" He started laughing and crying at the same time. He gave Steve a big hug. "Are you telling me that the President is going to give my good friend, Steve Bly, the Medal of Honor?"

Steve just nodded.

Michelle jumped up and hugged him, then Chelsea.

"Wild, white horses couldn't keep me from that ceremony—in the White House, right?" Jacob's eyes were bugged. He was shaking, almost bouncing.

"Calm down, cowboy. Yeah, the whole nine yards."

It was a beautiful morning in D.C. The Blys and the Andersons had breakfast with the President and his staff, at which they reviewed the procedures of the day.

At the ceremony, The President of the United States gave a heart-warming speech about Steve's career as a United States Marine and Navy SEAL.

"Having said all that," the President said, "I am honored today to award this medal to Commander Steve Bly for his heroic acts during a terrorist's attack on Port Aransas, Texas. After the helicopter he was in was blown out of the air and into the water, with broken ribs, arm and a leg, he still managed to pull two of his crewmen out of the wreckage before it sank. That, ladies and gentlemen, is an example for all future Marines to look up to. Therefore, if you will all rise for the occasion."

Steve Bly was a handsome man in his Marine Dress Blues. He stood perfectly still at ease, while the President spoke. But, when he turned to him, he snapped to a perfect position of attention. He clicked his heals, turned left face, face to face with the President of the United States.

The President took the Medal of Honor from his assistant and faced Steve.

Steve bent forward.

The President placed the ribbon around Steve's neck. Steve rose and saluted. The President returned the salute.

In the front row, Michelle, Paradise, and Chelsea were constantly wiping the tears. The women in Steve's life were very proud of him. Jacob stood silently awestruck at the spectacle.

ை • ஐ

The Andersons, all three, were honored at the state capitol by the Governor of Texas for their ongoing research and efforts to free captive dolphins.

Moreover, the whole family was awarded the Nobel Prize for Conservation—a new category initiated just for them.

Paradise went off to college, though we know not where.

Dolly had her baby—a little boy, Sam Jr.

Greg finished his novel.

The small Texas Coastal Bend town of Port Aransas fully recovered from the terrorist's attack, two fold.

It is amazing how God can bless those who follow Him and heed the call. Life was good.

And so the saga of Paradise, her family, and the dolphins lives on in Texas.

ABOUT THE AUTHOR

Born in Austin, Texas, Glenn Jacobson is a student of wildlife and marine mammals. His writing incorporates daily events and life-changing events with Biblical practices and spiritual views. His candor can be both serious and humorous. He is the writer and author of **Heaven by the Sea, Walking Through the Park, The Plight of Dolphins: When Humans Get in the Way, Paradise in Texas, Paradise: Dolphin Whisperer, Paradise: Sanctuary**, and **Old Friends Remembered**, as well as a collection of short stories called *Dog Tales*. He had articles published in both college newspapers and **The Smithville Times** as a contributing columnist. For three years, Mr. Jacobson conducted field research in non-point source pollution for the City of Austin, Texas, which led to his being named as *Co-Researcher* on a grant from the City of Austin with Dr. Steve Ziser (1993). He achieved membership into **Phi Theta Kappa, The National Deans List**, and **Who's Who in American Junior Colleges**. He was also accepted into **The Space Life Sciences Training Program (SLSTP)** at NASA's Kennedy Space Center (1992). His writing is inspirational and salty.